ACADEMIA NOTES

Ontario Security Guard Exam Study Guide

Complete Prep for the Ontario Licensing Test: PSISA, Arrest Powers, Use of Force, Emergencies, Report Writing + 2 Full Practice Exams (120 Questions) with Answer Key & Explanations

Academia
NOTES

First published by Academia Notes a division of Madole Labs 2025

First edition

ISBN: 978-1-0699763-0-7

This book was professionally typeset on Reedsy.
Find out more at reedsy.com

Contents

How to Use This Study Guide

This book is designed to help you prepare for the Ontario Security Guard licensing exam. It is written in clear, simple English and focuses on what you need to know for the test and for real security work.

Important: This Guide Does Not Replace Training

This book is a study guide to help you review and prepare for the Ontario Security Guard licensing exam. It is **not** a replacement for Ontario's required security guard training program, and it does **not** provide hands-on instruction (for example, physical skills, emergency drills, or workplace procedures). Always complete approved training, follow your employer's post orders, and follow current Ontario laws and licensing requirements.

You can use this guide in two main ways:

1. **Study from start to finish**, like a course.
2. **Use it as a review book**, focusing on the parts you find difficult.

What You Will Find in This Book

Each part of the book is organized to align with the topics covered in Ontario security guard training. Inside each chapter, you will find:

- Short explanations in plain language
- Key terms and important ideas
- "Exam Tips" that highlight common test traps

- Chapter summaries to help you review quickly
- Practice questions to check your understanding

How to Study (Simple Method)

Use this method to study efficiently:

1. **Read the chapter** once to understand the topic.
2. **Read it a second time** and highlight key points.
3. **Answer the practice questions** without looking at the answers.
4. **Check your answers** and review the explanations.
5. **Write down weak topics** to review again later.

Read the contents of this book slowly and take breaks. Understanding is more important than speed.

Recommended Study Plan

Most people can prepare in **7 to 14 days**, depending on the time available each day.

7-Day Plan (faster review)

- Day 1: Part 1 + Part 2 (Legal basics)
- Day 2: Use of Force + Arrest Powers
- Day 3: Emergency Response
- Day 4: Communication + De-escalation
- Day 5: Report Writing
- Day 6: Canadian Legal System + Review weak areas
- Day 7: Practice Exam #1 and #2 + final review

14-Day Plan (slower, more comfortable)

- Read one chapter per day
- Do practice questions daily
- Use the final 2 days for practice exams and review

How to Use Practice Exams

The practice exams are there to help you feel confident and ready.

To get the most value:

- Take the practice exam in a quiet place
- Set a timer
- Do not look at notes while writing
- Review every wrong answer and learn why it was wrong

If you score below your goal, do not worry. Use your results to guide what you study next.

Important Note About the Exam

This guide helps you prepare, but it is not an official government exam document. Laws and testing details can change over time. Always follow the current rules and training requirements in Ontario.

Final Tip

The exam is not only about memorizing facts. Many questions ask what a professional guard should do in a real situation. When you are unsure, choose the answer that is:

- **Safe**
- **Legal**
- **Professional**

- **Follows procedure**
- **Uses the least force necessary**

Ontario Security Guard Exam Overview

This section explains the Ontario Security Guard licensing exam in simple terms. Knowing how the exam works will help you study the right way and feel more confident on test day.

What the Exam Is

To become a licensed security guard in Ontario, you must complete approved training and then pass a provincial licensing exam. The exam assesses your understanding of the core topics covered in the required security guard training program.

This study guide is organized to match those topics.

Who the Exam Is For

The exam is for people who want to apply for an Ontario Security Guard licence. Many candidates are new to security work. You do not need previous security experience, but you do need to understand the rules, your limits, and what professional security guards are expected to do.

Exam Format (What to Expect)

Most candidates can expect the exam to be:

- **Multiple-choice**
- **Computer-based** (taken at a testing location)

- **Timed**
- Focused on real workplace situations, not just memorizing words

You will be asked to choose the best answer from several options. Some questions are straightforward. Others are scenario-based and test your judgment.

What the Exam Covers

The exam questions are based on the topics taught in Ontario's required training. These include:

- The role of a security guard and professionalism
- Basic legal concepts and limits of authority
- Powers of arrest and when a guard may act
- Use of force theory and safe decision-making
- Emergency response (fire, medical, and other incidents)
- Communication and conflict management
- Report writing and documentation
- Basic understanding of the Canadian legal system

This guide includes all of these areas, with review summaries and practice questions.

How Questions Are Often Written

Many questions ask what you should do first or what the best action is. When you are unsure, look for the answer that is:

- **Safe**
- **Legal**
- **Professional**
- **Follows site procedure**

- **Uses the least force necessary**
- **Calls for help when needed**

A common mistake is choosing an answer that sounds "tough" or "fast." In security work, the best answer is often the one that reduces risk and follows proper steps.

Common Exam Mistakes to Avoid

- Acting like a police officer
- Choosing force too quickly
- Detaining or searching without proper justification
- Ignoring safety (yours and others)
- Forgetting to report and document clearly
- Making decisions based on emotion instead of procedure

How This Book Helps You Pass

This guide is designed to help you learn faster and remember more. Each chapter includes:

- Plain-English explanations
- Key points and summaries
- Practice questions
- Exam-style tips and reminders

Use the practice questions to find weak areas early. Then review those sections again before writing the practice exams.

How the Licensing Process Works

This section outlines the steps to obtain a license as a security guard in Ontario. The process is not complicated, but you must complete each step in the correct order.

Step 1: Confirm You Meet Basic Requirements

Before you apply, make sure you meet the general requirements to work as a security guard in Ontario. These requirements may include age, identification, and eligibility to work in Canada.

If you are unsure about any requirement, check the official Ontario government licensing information to confirm the latest rules.

Step 2: Complete Approved Security Guard Training

You must complete an approved Ontario security guard training program. The training covers the topics that appear on the licensing exam, such as:

- Role of the security guard
- Legal authority and limitations
- Use of force theory
- Emergency response
- Communication and conflict management
- Report writing
- Basics of the Canadian legal system

After you complete the course, the training provider will issue proof of completion (typically a number or certificate). You will need this to book your exam.

Step 3: Book the Provincial Exam

After training, you must book the Ontario Security Guard licensing exam through the approved testing system. The exam is usually written at a test centre.

On exam day, you will need valid identification. Always follow the instructions provided when you book your exam.

Step 4: Write the Exam and Receive Your Result

You will write a multiple-choice exam. If you pass, you can move to the next step.

If you do not pass, you can usually rebook and retake the exam. Use your exam results and your practice test scores to focus your studying before your next attempt.

Step 5: Apply for Your Ontario Security Guard Licence

After you pass the exam, you can apply for your licence through the Ontario government. During the application, you will typically be asked for information such as:

- Personal identification details
- Proof of training and exam completion

- A photo (for the licence)
- Payment for licensing fees

Some applicants may also need to complete additional checks required by the licensing process.

Step 6: Receive Your Licence and Follow the Rules

Once your application is approved, you will receive your security guard licence. You must carry your licence (or have it available as required) while working.

Your licence comes with responsibilities. You must:

- Follow the Private Security and Investigative Services Act (PSISA)
- Follow the Ontario Code of Conduct for security guards
- Follow site post orders and employer procedures
- Act professionally and within your legal authority

Summary: Licensing Steps Checklist

- Meet basic requirements
- Complete approved training
- Book the provincial exam
- Pass the exam
- Apply for the licence
- Work legally and professionally

I

INTRODUCTION TO THE SECURITY INDUSTRY

Part 1 introduces security work in Ontario and what a security guard does. You'll learn the guard's main duties, what guards are not allowed to do, common places guards work, and the professional behaviour expected on the job and on the licensing exam.

1

The Role of a Security Guard in Ontario

A security guard's job is to protect people, property, and information by preventing problems when possible and responding professionally when issues occur. In Ontario, security guards work in the private security industry. This means they are hired by private employers or contracted to private clients, rather than employed by law enforcement.

A simple way to remember the core of the job is:
Deter. Observe. Report. Assist.

Most security duties fall under one (or more) of those four actions.

Role Clarity: What a Security Guard Is (and Is Not)

One of the most significant exam themes is understanding boundaries. A security guard is not a police officer and does not automatically have police powers. The security role is primarily concerned with prevention, safety, communication, and adherence to procedures.

A security guard generally does not:

- Investigate crimes the way police do
- Lay criminal charges
- Search people "because they feel like it."
- Detain someone without legal justification
- Use force as a first option

A guard's authority usually comes from two places:

1. The same rights and responsibilities as any private citizen
2. Acting as an agent of the property owner or employer (site rules and access control)

This is why good judgment matters. Security is about managing risk, not punishing people.

Core Responsibilities of a Security Guard

Prevention and Deterrence

Much of security is about reducing risk before an incident happens. A visible, professional guard presence can prevent theft, vandalism, and unsafe behaviour. Deterrence is not intimidation. It is a calm, consistent presence and routine.

Typical deterrence activities include patrolling, checking doors and vulnerable areas, monitoring cameras, controlling access, and watching for unusual patterns.

Observation and Awareness

Security guards are expected to notice what others might miss. Observation is more than "looking around." It means paying attention to behaviour, changes, and potential warning signs.

You may observe:

- **People:** agitation, intoxication, escalating conflict, suspicious behaviour
- **Places:** propped doors, blocked exits, damaged locks
- **Things:** unattended bags, tools that don't belong, missing assets
- **Patterns:** repeat problems, the same person returning, time-of-day trends

A professional guard stays alert without being reactive.

Reporting and Documentation

Reporting is one of the most critical parts of the job. Security work creates a record that may later be used by supervisors, employers, insurers, lawyers, or police. Transparent reporting also protects you, because it shows what you saw and what you did.

Reporting may include verbal updates, radio communications, logbook notes, and formal incident reports.

A strong report is:

- Accurate
- Objective
- Clear
- Complete
- Timely

A sound mindset is this: **if an incident wasn't documented properly, it becomes difficult to establish what happened.**

Customer Service and Public Interaction

Many security roles in Ontario are public-facing. Guards often provide directions, answer questions, and help maintain a calm environment. Being professional and respectful is part of the job.

In many workplaces, you are the first person visitors interact with. People may judge the entire organization by your attitude and behaviour.

Emergency Response (Within Your Role)

Security guards are often first on the scene in emergencies. Your goal is to help manage the situation safely until the proper resources arrive.

Depending on the site, you may respond to fire alarms, evacuations, medical situations, suspicious packages, equipment failures, or aggressive behaviour.

In emergencies, avoid the "hero" mindset. Focus on safety and procedure:

- Keep yourself safe
- Protect others when possible
- Call for appropriate help early
- Follow site procedures
- Document what occurred

Common Work Settings in Ontario

Security guards work in many environments. The setting changes, but the core role remains the same.

Examples include:

- Retail and malls (theft prevention, customer conflict)
- Corporate offices (access control, visitor management)
- Warehouses and industrial sites (perimeter security, safety hazards)

- Construction sites (after-hours patrol, asset protection)
- Hospitals and healthcare sites (high stress, sensitive situations)
- Events and venues (crowds, intoxication issues, emergencies)
- Residential buildings (concierge-style security, disputes, parking issues)

On the exam, questions may describe a scenario. Your best approach is to consider what your role permits and what the safest, most professional response would be.

Authority and Limitations: The Big Picture

Many exam questions test whether you understand the difference between what you can do and what you should do.

In general, a security guard can:

- Enforce site rules (as the property owner's agent)
- Ask someone to identify themselves (a person may refuse)
- Ask someone to leave private property
- Call the police and provide accurate information
- Take reasonable steps to protect people and property when necessary, within the law and training

In general, a security guard cannot:

- Force identification just because they want it
- Search someone without lawful grounds, consent, or applicable policy conditions
- Detain someone without proper legal justification
- Use force to make someone obey, to punish, or to "teach a lesson."
- Impersonate police or suggest they have police powers

A professional guard manages risk and escalates appropriately when a situation is beyond their authority.

Working with Police (and When to Call)

Security guards and police may collaborate, but their roles differ. Police investigate crimes and enforce criminal law. Guards observe, preserve safety, and report.

You should call the police (or emergency services) when:

- Violence has occurred or is likely
- A crime is in progress or has just happened
- Someone needs urgent medical assistance
- Weapons are involved or suspected
- You feel unsafe or outmatched
- The incident exceeds your training or site procedures

When police arrive, your value is in clear information: **what happened, where it happened, when it happened, who was involved, and what you observed.**

Professionalism: What the Exam Expects

Professionalism is not merely about politeness. It includes:

- Respectful communication
- Neutral, calm behaviour under stress
- Honesty and accuracy in reporting
- Confidentiality with sensitive information
- Following site rules and lawful instructions
- Knowing your limits and calling for help when appropriate

A common mistake is focusing on "winning" an argument. In security, success usually means resolving an issue safely, without escalation.

Safety Mindset: Your Most Important Tool

Security work involves risk. A strong guard uses basic risk assessment before acting.

Ask yourself: **What is the threat? Do I have a safe exit? Am I alone? Do I need backup? What does the site procedure require? Is there a safer option than getting physically involved?**

As a rule, communication and procedure are preferable to physical action, unless there is an immediate need to ensure safety.

Chapter 1 Summary

You should now understand:

- A security guard's purpose is to **deter, observe, report, and assist**
- Guards are **not police** and have **limited authority**
- Prevention, awareness, and documentation are key job skills
- Customer service and professionalism are part of security work
- Safety-first decision-making and proper escalation are essential

* * *

Quick Check: Practice Questions (Chapter 1)

1) The primary purpose of a security guard is to:

A. Arrest offenders

B. Deter, observe, report, and assist

C. Investigate crimes

D. Lay charges

2) A security guard's authority on a site mainly comes from:

A. Police powers

B. Court orders

C. Private citizen authority and acting for the property owner/employer

D. The Criminal Code gives guards special status

3) The best general first step in a potential incident is to:

A. Use force to gain control

B. Observe and assess, then follow the procedure

C. Immediately detain the person

D. Confiscate property

Answers:

1) B

2) C

3) B

2

Professionalism and Ethics

Professionalism is one of the most important parts of security work in Ontario. It affects safety, the public's trust, and your employer's reputation. It also affects your licence. Many exam questions are based on situations where a guard must choose the most professional and ethical response.

In security work, professionalism means more than being polite. It means you act in a way that is safe, legal, fair, and respectful—especially when people are upset, angry, or difficult.

Code of Conduct Under PSISA

Ontario security guards are expected to follow a professional code of conduct. The purpose of the code is to help guards act responsibly and to protect the public.

A professional security guard should:

- Act honestly and with integrity
- Treat people fairly and with respect
- Use only the force that is reasonable and necessary (and only when required)

- Avoid discrimination, harassment, and abusive language
- Respect privacy and keep information confidential
- Follow the law, employer policies, and site procedures
- Cooperate with the police when appropriate
- Avoid pretending to be a police officer or claiming police powers

The exam may test your understanding of the code through scenarios. You may be asked what a guard should do, what a guard should not do, or what behaviour is most professional.

Ethical Behaviour

Ethics means doing the right thing, even when nobody is watching. Ethical behaviour builds trust with the public, your employer, and your team. It also protects you, because poor decisions can lead to complaints, job loss, or licensing problems.

Ethical behaviour includes:

- Being truthful in reports and statements
- Doing your job without using your position for personal gain
- Treating all people equally and respectfully
- Staying calm and professional under pressure
- Not escalating situations because of pride, anger, or embarrassment
- Following procedures even when it is inconvenient

A common security mistake is reacting emotionally. If someone insults you or challenges you, the professional response is to remain calm, follow procedure, and prioritize safety.

Confidentiality and Privacy

Security guards often see private information. You might learn details about customers, employees, visitors, or business operations. You may also see camera footage, incident reports, or sensitive site information.

Confidentiality means:

- Do not share information with friends, family, or on social media
- Do not discuss incidents publicly
- Do not share photos, videos, or names of people involved
- Only share information with people who are authorized to receive it (such as your supervisor, client contact, or police when appropriate)

Even casual sharing can cause harm. It can also damage trust and create legal problems for you and your employer.

Conflicts of Interest

A conflict of interest happens when your personal interests could affect your professional judgment. Even if you do not intend to do anything wrong, a conflict of interest can make people question your honesty and fairness.

Common examples include:

- Accepting money or gifts in exchange for "help" or special treatment
- Doing favours for friends or family while on duty
- Ignoring rule-breaking because you know the person
- Using your position to gain personal benefits (discounts, free items, special access)
- Working a side job creates a problem with your main job or client

If you encounter a conflict of interest, the best course of action is usually to report it to your supervisor and follow their instructions. Your goal is to stay neutral and protect your integrity.

Appearance, Attitude, and Accountability

A security guard's appearance and attitude affect how people respond to them. A professional guard is more likely to de-escalate situations than to escalate them.

Professional appearance and behaviour include:

- Wearing the proper uniform and identification
- Being clean, neat, and prepared for the shift
- Arriving on time and staying alert
- Using professional language (no swearing, insults, or threats)
- Speaking calmly and clearly
- Following post orders and site policies
- Taking responsibility for mistakes and reporting issues honestly

Accountability entails understanding that your actions matter. Even small decisions can have serious outcomes. A professional guard can explain their actions clearly and demonstrate that they followed the procedure and acted in good faith.

Professional Communication and Respect

Security work involves dealing with many different people. You may interact with customers, employees, visitors, contractors, and people who are upset or intoxicated.

Professional communication means:

- Use respectful language

- Listen before reacting
- Give clear and simple instructions
- Avoid arguing or making threats
- Maintain a calm tone and controlled body language
- Keep a safe distance and watch for warning signs
- Call for backup early when needed

Respect does not imply agreement with someone. It means treating them fairly and avoiding unnecessary escalation.

Exam Focus: Scenario-Based Ethics Questions

Many exam questions are framed as short workplace scenarios. To choose the best answer, ask yourself:

- Is it safe?
- Is it legal?
- Is it professional?
- Does it follow the procedure?
- Does it treat people fairly and respectfully?
- Would I be comfortable explaining this decision to my supervisor later?

In most ethics questions, the correct answer is the one that protects safety, respects rights, avoids escalation, and follows policy. Be careful with answers that sound "tough" or "fast." In security work, the best response is often calm, controlled, and procedure-based.

Chapter 2 Summary

You should now understand:

- Professionalism is required in Ontario security work and is tested on the exam

- Ethical behaviour includes honesty, fairness, confidentiality, and self-control
- Conflicts of interest can damage trust and must be avoided or reported
- Appearance and attitude influence safety and public cooperation
- Scenario questions usually reward the safest, most professional, and procedure-based choice

* * *

Quick Check: Practice Questions (Chapter 2)

1) A visitor insults you and refuses to follow a rule. What is the most professional response?

A. Insult them back to show authority
B. Stay calm, explain the rule clearly, and follow the site procedure
C. Physically remove them immediately
D. Threaten to arrest them

2) A friend asks you to "let them in" without signing in because it's late. What should you do?

A. Let them in because you know them
B. Let them in if they promise to sign in later
C. Follow the standard access procedure or contact your supervisor for direction
D. Ignore the situation

3) Which is an example of a conflict of interest?

A. Writing an incident report
B. Treating everyone equally

C. Accepting a gift in exchange for ignoring a rule violation

D. Calling police when needed

4) You witnessed an incident at work. What is the most ethical approach to reporting it?

A. Leave out details to avoid trouble

B. Exaggerate details to make your report stronger

C. Write an accurate, objective report with facts only

D. Wait a few days and write it from memory

Answers:

1) B

2) C

3) C

4) C

II

LEGAL STUDIES & AUTHORITY

Part 2 explains the laws and legal limits that apply to Ontario security guards. You'll learn about PSISA, powers of arrest, trespass issues, search and detention rules, and use of force theory. This section focuses on what you can and cannot do, how to act legally and safely, and how to answer scenario-based exam questions.

3

The Private Security and Investigative Services Act (PSISA)

The Private Security and Investigative Services Act (PSISA) is one of the most significant statutes governing security guards in Ontario. It establishes the rules governing who may work as a security guard, how guards must behave, and what security businesses must do to operate lawfully.

Many exam questions are based on PSISA. The most common focus is on the distinction between what a guard is permitted to do and what a guard is prohibited from doing.

Purpose of PSISA

PSISA exists to protect the public and create professional standards in the private security industry. It helps ensure that security guards and private investigators are trained, licensed, and accountable.

In simple terms, PSISA is meant to:

- Set minimum standards for training and licensing
- Regulate security guard behaviour through rules and a Code of Conduct

- Prevent unlicensed people from working as guards
- Ensure guards and employers can be held responsible for misconduct
- Build public trust in the security industry

If you remember one thing, remember this: **PSISA is about regulation and professionalism.**

Licensing Requirements

In Ontario, you must have a valid security guard licence to work as a security guard. Working without a licence (or using someone else's licence) is a serious issue.

Licensing rules include:

- You must meet Ontario's eligibility requirements
- You must complete approved training
- You must pass the licensing exam
- You must apply for a licence and keep it valid (renew when required)
- You must follow the Code of Conduct and legal requirements while working

Your licence is not just a piece of ID. It demonstrates that you are legally authorized to perform the job and that you are expected to meet professional standards.

Duties and Responsibilities Under PSISA

PSISA does not give security guards "police powers." Instead, it sets expectations and limits. It supports the view that security guards must work professionally and comply with the law.

Your responsibilities as a licensed guard include:

- Acting honestly and professionally
- Following the Code of Conduct
- Following the law and employer/site procedures
- Identifying yourself correctly when required
- Avoiding actions that mislead the public (for example, acting like police)
- Reporting incidents accurately and objectively
- Using only reasonable force when necessary and lawful

A key examination principle is that **PSISA defines standards and restrictions, not special powers.**

Uniforms, Identification, and Badges

PSISA includes rules about how security guards present themselves. This is important because the public must be able to distinguish between a security guard and a police officer.

As a security guard, you may be required to:

- Wear a uniform if the job requires it
- Carry your licence while working
- Show your licence or identification when required by law or policy
- Follow rules about badges, patches, or identification cards

A security guard must not present themselves in a way that confuses the public. For example, a guard must not use symbols, clothing, or behaviour that suggests they are police.

On the exam, if you see a question about uniforms or badges, the safest answer is usually the one that emphasizes:

- Clear identification as a security guard
- No police-like appearance or claims

- Following employer policy and legal standards

Offences Under PSISA

An offence is a serious violation of the law. PSISA includes offences for both individuals and businesses. The exam often tests your ability to recognize clearly illegal behaviour.

Examples of actions that can lead to offences include:

- Working as a security guard without a valid licence
- Using someone else's licence or allowing someone to use yours
- Providing false information during licensing or investigations
- Failing to follow the required standards and rules
- Pretending to be police or using police-like identifiers to mislead the public
- Employers using unlicensed guards or operating improperly

Remember: PSISA is not just "rules." It has consequences. A guard who breaks PSISA can face penalties and may lose the ability to work in the industry.

Exam Focus: What PSISA Allows vs. Prohibits

Many PSISA exam questions can be answered by using a simple checklist. When you are unsure, ask:

- Is the person appropriately licensed to do this work?
- Does the behaviour match professional standards and the Code of Conduct?
- Is the guard clearly identified as a security guard (not a police officer)?
- Is the guard acting within the law, policy, and their role?
- Would this behaviour mislead the public or abuse authority?

In most cases, the correct exam answer will be the one that supports licensing, professionalism, honesty, and clear identification.

Chapter 3 Summary

You should now understand:

- PSISA regulates the private security industry in Ontario and protects the public
- Security guards must be licensed and must follow professional standards
- PSISA focuses on duties, conduct, and restrictions—not special police powers
- Uniform and identification rules exist to prevent confusion with the police
- PSISA includes offences for unlicensed work, dishonesty, and misconduct
- Many exam questions test what PSISA allows versus what it prohibits

* * *

Quick Check: Practice Questions (Chapter 3)

1) The main purpose of PSISA is to:

A. Give security guards police powers
B. Regulate the private security industry and protect the public
C. Allow guards to search anyone on private property
D. Replace the Criminal Code

2) Which action is most clearly prohibited under PSISA principles?

A. Wearing required identification
B. Writing an objective incident report
C. Presenting yourself in a way that confuses the public into thinking you

are police

D. Following site procedures

3) Which statement is correct?

A. A licence is optional if you have experience

B. A guard can work without a licence if supervised

C. A guard must have a valid licence to work as a security guard in Ontario

D. A licence is only needed for event security

4) PSISA is mainly about:

A. Regulating training, licensing, and professional conduct

B. Teaching self-defence techniques

C. Giving guards authority to detain anyone

D. Replacing employer policies

Answers:

1) B

2) C

3) C

4) A

4

Powers of Arrest

Understanding arrest powers is one of the most important topics for Ontario security guards. The exam often tests whether you know what a guard can do, what a guard cannot do, and what a guard should do in everyday situations.

Security guards do not have special police powers. In most cases, a security guard's arrest authority derives from the same source as that of any private citizen.

Citizen's Arrest vs. Police Arrest

A **police officer** conducts an arrest under the authority granted by law. Police also have broader authority to investigate crimes, detain individuals, and exercise certain powers during investigations.

A **citizen's arrest** is an arrest made by a private person (including a security guard). A citizen's arrest is more limited. It is not meant to replace police work. It is intended for specific situations and must be performed carefully.

As a security guard, your primary role is usually to:

- Observe and assess

- Keep people safe
- Call the police early when needed
- Follow the site procedure
- Document what happened

Arrest is an option only in certain situations. It is not the default response.

Section 494 of the Criminal Code

In Canada, the main rule for citizens' arrest is found in **Section 494 of the Criminal Code**. This section is often mentioned in Ontario security guard training and is a common exam topic.

Section 494 is important because it explains when a private person may arrest someone. It also helps define when an arrest would be unlawful.

You do not need to memorize the exact wording for the exam, but you do need to understand the basic idea:

- A private person may arrest someone in limited circumstances, typically when a crime is occurring or has just occurred, and certain conditions are met.

If you are unsure, the safest course is often to **call the police and serve as a reliable witness** rather than attempt an arrest.

When a Guard May Arrest

A security guard may arrest in certain situations, such as:

- When a person is caught committing a criminal offence (for example, theft)
- When the situation meets the conditions for a citizen's arrest under

Section 494

- When the arrest can be done safely and reasonably
- When site procedures support the action, and you can explain your decision, step-by-step

In real-world security work, arrests often occur in situations such as retail theft, trespassing, or property damage. However, even when a guard arrests, the guard must still consider safety and necessity.

Before making an arrest, a professional guard considers:

- Is there an immediate risk to people or severe property damage?
- Do I have enough facts, or am I guessing?
- Can I manage this safely, or do I need the police?
- Do I have backup?
- Is there a safer option, such as observation and police involvement?

A lawful arrest can still be a bad decision if it is unsafe or unnecessary.

When a Guard Must Not Arrest

There are also times when a guard must not arrest. A guard should not arrest when:

- They did not personally see what happened and have no reliable facts
- The situation does not meet the requirements for a citizen's arrest
- The person is only breaking a site rule (not committing a criminal offence)
- The risk of harm is high (for example, weapons suspected, a large group, an unsafe environment)
- The guard is acting out of anger, embarrassment, or revenge
- The guard is using arrest to punish or "teach a lesson."

A common theme in standard exams is that security guards should not "stretch" their authority. If the situation is unclear, it is usually better to observe, call the police, and document what happened.

What to Do After an Arrest (High-Level)

If a guard makes an arrest, the following steps should focus on safety and proper procedure. This will vary by employer and site, but general principles include:

- Call the police as soon as possible
- Use only reasonable force if needed for safety
- Do not argue or escalate
- Monitor the person for medical distress
- Do not search unless lawful and permitted by policy (and only within your authority)
- Document everything clearly and factually

This topic connects to other chapters, especially the use of force, communication, and report writing.

Common Arrest Mistakes

Many legal problems for guards arise from avoidable mistakes. The exam often tests these.

Common mistakes include:

- Arresting without proper legal grounds
- Arresting because of suspicion instead of facts
- Confusing site policy violations with criminal offences
- Using too much force or escalating the situation
- Failing to call the police quickly after an arrest
- Poor documentation (missing details, opinions, or exaggerations)

- Detaining someone "to ask questions" without lawful justification
- Making statements that suggest you are the police or have police authority

A good security guard is careful and controlled. The goal is always safety and legality, not control for its own sake.

EXAM TIP: One of the Most Tested Topics

Questions about arrest powers often include tricky wording. To avoid common traps:

- Remember that security guards do not have automatic police powers
- Citizen's arrest is limited and must meet specific conditions
- When uncertain, the safest professional action is usually to **observe, call the police, and report**
- Look for answers that emphasize safety, legality, and procedure
- Avoid answers that sound aggressive, emotional, or "punishment-focused."

Chapter 4 Summary

You should now understand:

- A security guard's arrest power is usually the same as a private citizen's arrest power
- Police have broader authority than security guards
- Section 494 of the Criminal Code is the key rule behind a citizen's arrest
- Guards must know when an arrest is permitted and when it is not
- Most arrest mistakes involve poor judgment, unclear grounds, unsafe action, or bad reporting
- Exam questions often test what you should do first, and whether an arrest is lawful and reasonable

* * *

Quick Check: Practice Questions (Chapter 4)

1) Which statement best describes a security guard's arrest authority in Ontario?

A. Security guards have the same arrest powers as police while on duty

B. Security guards can arrest anyone who refuses to follow site rules

C. Security guards usually rely on the same citizen's arrest powers as private citizens

D. Security guards can arrest only if a supervisor approves it

2) Which situation is the best example of when a guard should NOT arrest?

A. You directly observe a person committing theft, and it is safe to act

B. You suspect someone stole an item earlier, but you did not see it happen

C. You catch a person damaging property, and the police are not yet on scene

D. A person is actively assaulting someone, and immediate action is required for safety

3) If you make an arrest, what is the correct next step in most cases?

A. Call the police as soon as possible and follow the site procedure

B. Delay calling the police until you have questioned the person

C. Search the person automatically for evidence

D. Post the details on social media to warn others

4) Which is a common arrest mistake?

A. Documenting what happened in a factual report

B. Keeping a safe distance and calling the police when needed

C. Making an arrest based only on suspicion, without clear legal grounds

D. Following post orders and supervisor direction

Answers:

1) C

2) B

3) A

4) C

5

Use of Force Theory

Use of force is a topic every security guard must understand clearly. It affects safety, legality, and your licence. This chapter explains how to choose the least forceful option that works, and when force is not justified.

Use of Force Continuum

A use-of-force continuum is a simple way to understand how responses should match the situation. It is not a permission slip to "move up" to a higher force. Instead, it helps guards think about options and choose the safest, least forceful response that will work.

Common levels on a continuum include:

- **Officer presence:** your visible, professional presence may prevent problems
- **Verbal communication:** clear instructions, calm tone, de-escalation
- **Soft physical control:** minimal physical guidance or restraint (only if lawful and necessary)
- **Hard physical control:** stronger physical techniques (higher risk, only if required and lawful)
- **Defensive tools or higher force:** generally outside the role of most guards

and highly restricted

The exact names may vary by training provider. Still, the exam focuses on the main idea: **start with the lowest effective option and use higher levels only when needed for safety.**

Reasonable vs. Excessive Force

A key exam word is **reasonable**. Reasonable force means the amount of force necessary and appropriate in the circumstances. It must match the threat and stop when the threat stops.

Excessive force is force that is more than what is necessary. It can happen when:

- A guard uses force when there is no real threat
- A guard uses more force than needed to control the situation
- A guard continues using force after the person is controlled
- A guard uses force as punishment or "to teach a lesson."
- A guard escalates force because they are angry or embarrassed

A professional guard uses force only to protect safety, and only as long as needed.

Situational Assessment

Situational assessment is the process of quickly evaluating the situation and selecting the safest response. It is one of the most critical skills in security work.

Before acting, assess:

- **Threat level:** Is anyone in immediate danger?

- **Behaviour:** Is the person calm, upset, aggressive, or violent?
- **Weapons:** Are weapons present or suspected?
- **Environment:** Is the area crowded? Are there exits? Is there cover?
- **Backup:** Are you alone? Can you call for help?
- **Your role:** What does the law allow? What do post orders require?

In many situations, the best choice is to create space, communicate calmly, call the police, and observe. Physical action increases risk and should be avoided unless necessary for safety.

Duty of Care

Security guards have a **duty of care**, which means they must act reasonably to help prevent harm. This includes protecting people on the property, following procedures, and making decisions that reduce risk.

Duty of care does **not** mean you must put yourself in danger. It means you must make responsible choices, including calling the right help when needed.

Practical examples of duty of care include:

- Not escalating situations unnecessarily
- Calling police or emergency services when appropriate
- Monitoring for medical distress when an incident occurs
- Writing accurate, objective reports after the event

Legal Consequences of Misuse

Misusing force can lead to serious consequences, even if a guard believes they were "trying to help." Misuse may result in:

- **Criminal consequences** (for example, assault-related charges)
- **Civil consequences** (being sued)

- **Employment consequences** (discipline or termination)
- **Licensing consequences** (complaints, suspension, or loss of licence)

This is why force decisions must be based on safety, law, and necessity—not emotion.

Exam Focus: Reasonableness and Proportionality

Two words appear often in exam-style questions:

- **Reasonableness:** Was the action justified and sensible in the circumstances?
- **Proportionality:** Did the response match the level of threat?

When you are unsure, choose the option that protects safety, follows procedure, uses communication first when possible, and uses the least force necessary.

Chapter 5 Summary

You should now understand:

- The use of force continuum helps match response to threat, starting with the least forceful effective option
- Reasonable force is necessary and appropriate; excessive force is more than needed or used for too long
- Situational assessment helps you choose safer options and avoid escalation
- Duty of care means acting reasonably to prevent harm while following procedure
- Misuse of force can lead to criminal, civil, employment, and licensing consequences
- Exam questions often test reasonableness and proportionality in real

scenarios

* * *

Quick Check: Practice Questions (Chapter 5)

1) What does "proportionality" mean in use-of-force decisions?

A. The response should match the level of threat

B. The response should always include physical control

C. The response should continue until the person apologizes

D. The response should be the same in every incident

2) Which situation is most likely to be considered excessive force?

A. Creating distance and calling for help when a person becomes aggressive

B. Using minimal force to protect someone from immediate harm

C. Giving clear verbal directions and documenting the incident

D. Continuing to use force after the person is controlled and no longer a threat

3) The use-of-force continuum is best described as:

A. A rule that requires force whenever someone refuses to cooperate

B. A guide to help choose the least forceful effective response based on the situation

C. A permission slip to increase force when you feel disrespected

D. A replacement for post orders and site procedures

4) Duty of care means a security guard should:

A. Avoid calling the police to keep incidents quiet

B. Physically intervene in every situation to show effort

C. Act reasonably to prevent harm, follow procedure, and get help when needed

D. Use force quickly to end incidents faster

Answers:

1) A

2) D

3) B

4) C

6

Search, Detention, and Seizure

Security guards often encounter situations involving individuals suspected of theft, carrying prohibited items, or violating site rules. In these moments, it is easy to make mistakes—especially with searching and detaining. This chapter explains what security guards can and cannot do, and how to handle these situations professionally and legally.

A good rule to remember is this: **security guards do not have automatic search powers.** In most cases, searching or detaining a person without proper authority can create serious legal problems.

When Searches Are Permitted

Searches are only permitted in certain situations. The exact rules can depend on the site type, employer policies, and the circumstances of the incident. The most common lawful basis for a security guard search is **consent**.

In general, a security guard may be able to search when:

- The person **voluntarily agrees** to the search (consent)
- The search is connected to a lawful and clearly stated **site policy** (for example, entry conditions at specific workplaces)

- The search is necessary for **immediate safety** in a serious situation and aligns with lawful authority and procedure
- Police are present and direct particular actions within their authority (the guard should still follow policy and only assist appropriately)

In most public-facing security roles, the safest and most common approach is to **ask for consent; if permission is refused, follow site procedure and consider calling the police.**

Consent Searches

A consent search means the person agrees to be searched. Consent must be honest and voluntary. If someone agrees only because they feel threatened or forced, the consent may not be valid.

Good practice for consent searches includes:

- Explain the request clearly and calmly
- Keep your tone professional (no threats or insults)
- Give the person a choice
- If they refuse, do not escalate—follow procedure

A simple example of professional wording is:
"Site policy requires a bag check to enter. If you do not want a search, you may choose not to enter."

Consent can also be withdrawn. If someone says "stop," the search should stop, and you should follow your site's procedure.

Private Property Rights

Private property owners can set rules for access and behaviour on their property. Security guards often enforce these rules as agents of the property owner or employer. This is why many sites have rules like:

- No weapons
- No alcohol
- Bags may be subject to inspection
- Certain areas are restricted
- Visitors must sign in and show ID

These are **site rules**, not criminal law. A person can usually choose to follow the rule or leave the property. If the person refuses to comply and go, the situation may escalate into a trespass issue, and police may need to be involved.

A key point of the exam is this: **site rules are not the same as legal authority to search or detain.** Guards enforce site rules, but they must still respect the law and act reasonably.

Detention: What It Means and When It May Happen

Detention means keeping someone from leaving. Detaining someone is serious. If a guard detains someone without legal justification, it can lead to legal consequences (for example, a complaint, civil lawsuit, or criminal issues).

In many workplaces, guards use "detention" loosely when they really mean "asking someone to wait." Those are not the same thing.

- Asking someone to wait is voluntary. They can refuse and leave.
- Detention means the person is not free to leave.

A guard should only detain when there is a clear lawful basis, such as circumstances connected to a lawful arrest. When unsure, the safer professional choice is usually to observe, call the police, and document.

What Security Guards Cannot Seize

Security guards may discover property suspected of being stolen or prohibited. However, "seizing" property is not something a guard can do freely.

In many situations, a guard cannot:

- Take property from someone just because they suspect it is stolen
- Confiscate items as punishment
- Keep personal property without lawful authority and clear policy direction
- Search a person to find property unless the search is lawful and permitted

If property must be handled, follow the site procedure. In some cases, police should be called to handle evidence or stolen items properly.

Evidence Handling Basics

Security guards are not forensic investigators. Still, how you handle information and items matters; good evidence handling protects the integrity of the situation and supports police or employer investigations later.

Basic best practices include:

- Write down facts as soon as possible (times, locations, names, descriptions)
- Keep notes objective (what you saw and heard, not opinions)
- Preserve video footage whenever possible by reporting it promptly to the appropriate person.
- Avoid unnecessary handling of items connected to an incident

- If items must be handled, follow the site procedure and document what you did

Evidence handling is strongly connected to report writing. A clear, factual report often becomes the most important "evidence" a guard creates.

Chapter 6 Summary

You should now understand:

- Searches by security guards are limited and are often based on consent and site policy
- Consent must be voluntary, and a person can refuse or withdraw consent
- Private property rules allow a site to set conditions of entry, but this does not give unlimited search powers
- Detention is serious and must have a lawful justification
- Security guards cannot seize property freely; follow procedure and involve police when appropriate
- Good evidence handling includes accurate notes, preserving information, and minimizing unnecessary handling

* * *

Quick Check: Practice Questions (Chapter 6)

1) A visitor refuses a bag check required by site policy. What is the most appropriate response?

A. Search the bag anyway because it is private property

B. Explain the policy and deny entry or request the person to leave, following site procedure

C. Detain the person until they agree

D. Confiscate the bag and hold it at the desk

2) What is a key requirement of a consent search?

A. The person must agree voluntarily and can refuse

B. The guard must be wearing a uniform

C. The guard must have a supervisor present

D. The guard must already have detained the person

3) Which statement best describes "detention"?

A. Asking someone a question

B. Writing an incident report

C. Keeping someone from leaving when they are not free to go

D. Watching someone on camera

4) Which is an example of good evidence handling?

A. Handling items as little as possible and documenting facts clearly

B. Posting details online to warn the community

C. Taking suspected stolen items as punishment

D. Waiting until the end of the week to write notes

Answers:

1) B

2) A

3) C

4) A

III

Emergency Response

Part 3 teaches how to respond to emergencies safely and professionally. You'll learn what to do during fires, evacuations, bomb threats, medical emergencies, and other critical incidents. This section focuses on staying calm, protecting people, calling the right help early, following site procedures, and documenting what happened.

7

Emergency Situations

Emergencies are stressful and fast-moving. A professional security guard remains calm, adheres to procedures, and prioritizes safety. In most emergencies, your role is not to "solve" the event alone. Your role is to **respond safely**, obtain appropriate assistance **early**, and **support an organized response**.

This chapter covers common emergencies that security guards may encounter on duty and the basic steps expected of them in Ontario.

Fires and Evacuations

Fire response is one of the most common emergency responsibilities for security guards. Fires can spread quickly and create smoke, panic, and confusion. Your job is to help people get to safety and to support the site's emergency plan.

In a fire situation, priorities usually follow this order:

1. **Life safety:** protect people first
2. **Call for help:** activate alarms and contact emergency services as required
3. **Evacuation:** support safe and orderly evacuation
4. **Information:** communicate clear directions and report key details

5. **Documentation:** record what happened after the situation is controlled

A few practical points that often matter:

- Do not assume an alarm is "false." Treat alarms seriously until confirmed otherwise.
- Never block exits or allow evacuation routes to become cluttered.
- Do not use elevators during most fire evacuations unless the site procedure says otherwise.
- If smoke is present, keep low and avoid entering hazardous areas.
- Only attempt firefighting if you are trained, it is safe, and the site policy allows it.

Once people are out, help direct them to the assembly area. Do not allow re-entry until the proper authority confirms it is safe.

Bomb Threats

Bomb threats can arrive by phone, email, letter, or in person. Many threats are unfounded, but every threat must be taken seriously and addressed calmly.

If you receive a bomb threat by phone, your goals are to **remain calm**, **collect information**, and **notify the appropriate authorities**. If safe to do so, try to note:

- Exact words used by the caller
- Any background sounds (traffic, voices, music)
- Caller tone, accent, or speech patterns
- Whether the caller mentions a location, time, or reason

Do not argue with the caller. Keep them talking only as long as it is safe and realistic.

After the threat:

- Follow the site procedure immediately
- Notify your supervisor and the designated site contact
- Contact the police as required
- Do not use radios or phones near a suspicious item if the site procedure warns against it.
- Do not touch or move suspicious items

The site's emergency plan will guide whether evacuation or other actions are required. Always follow the plan.

Suspicious Packages

A suspicious package is any item that seems out of place or has warning signs. It might be a bag left unattended, a box in an unusual location, or an item with strange features. Not all suspicious packages are dangerous, but the risk must be managed carefully.

Warning signs can include:

- No owner nearby and unusual location
- Strange odour, stains, or leaking
- Wires, ticking sounds, or unusual protrusions
- Excessive tape, strange labelling, or threats written on it

If you find a suspicious package, remember this simple rule: **do not touch it.**

Typical safe steps are:

- Clear people away and create distance
- Notify supervisor/site contact
- Call police or emergency services as required

- Follow site instructions for isolation and evacuation
- Document what you observed (location, appearance, time discovered)

Active Threat Awareness

Active threats may include violence, weapons, or a situation where people are at immediate risk. In these events, personal safety is critical. Security guards are not expected to act like police. Your role is to support safety and an organized response.

A helpful way to think about active threats is:

- **Get to safety if possible**
- **Warn others**
- **Call emergency services**
- **Provide clear information**

Your actions depend on the site procedure and the situation, but most exam questions will reward answers that focus on:

- Protecting yourself and others
- Creating distance from danger
- Calling the police early
- Not attempting risky intervention beyond your training

Lockdown Procedures

A lockdown is implemented when there is a serious threat, and it is safer for people to remain in secure areas rather than evacuate. Lockdowns are common in schools, healthcare, and large facilities, but many workplaces have lockdown procedures as part of their emergency plan.

In a lockdown, your role may include:

- Following the site's lockdown procedure exactly
- Helping secure doors or access points if it is safe
- Directing people to safe areas
- Communicating updates clearly and calmly
- Keeping unauthorized people from entering restricted areas
- Relaying information to the police or the site contact

During a lockdown, avoid spreading rumours. Share only confirmed information through proper channels. When the lockdown ends, it should be lifted only by the appropriate authority in accordance with procedure.

Exam Focus: Order of Response and Personal Safety

Emergency questions on the exam often ask what you should do first. When you are unsure, use this priority order:

1. **Personal safety and life safety**
2. **Call the right help early** (911, fire, police, medical, supervisor)
3. **Follow site procedure** (emergency plan, post orders)
4. **Support control and communication** (clear directions, calm presence)
5. **Document facts** after the incident is stabilized

Avoid answers that involve taking unnecessary risks, touching suspicious items, or delaying emergency calls.

Chapter 7 Summary

You should now understand:

- Fire response focuses on life safety, alarms, evacuation support, and following the procedure
- Bomb threats must be treated seriously; collect information and notify properly

- Suspicious packages should not be touched; create distance and call for help
- Active threat response prioritizes safety, warning others, and contacting police
- Lockdown procedures are site-specific and must be followed exactly
- Exam questions often test the order of response and personal safety choices

* * *

Quick Check: Practice Questions (Chapter 7)

1) You discover an unattended bag in a restricted area with wires visible. What should you do first?

A. Open the bag to confirm what it is

B. Move the bag to a safer location

C. Create distance and keep people away, then notify according to procedure

D. Take a photo and post it to warn others

2) During a fire alarm, what is the most appropriate general approach?

A. Treat it as a false alarm unless smoke is visible

B. Support life safety and evacuation procedures, and follow the site emergency plan

C. Lock all exits to prevent theft during evacuation

D. Wait for a supervisor before taking any action

3) If you receive a bomb threat by phone, your best goal is to:

A. Stay calm, collect details, and notify the right people immediately after the call

B. Hang up quickly to end the threat

C. Argue with the caller to prove you are not afraid

D. Announce the threat publicly to the building right away without procedure

4) Which statement best describes the purpose of a lockdown?

A. To evacuate people as quickly as possible

B. To keep operations running normally during emergencies

C. To bring all visitors to the reception for questioning

D. To keep people secured inside safe areas, leaving may be more dangerous

Answers:

1) C

2) B

3) A

4) D

8

Medical Emergencies

Medical emergencies can happen anywhere: a visitor faints, an employee has chest pain, a customer has a severe allergic reaction, or someone is injured in a fall. In many workplaces, a security guard is among the first individuals notified. Your role is to respond calmly, seek assistance promptly, and support a safe, organized response.

This chapter covers basic first-aid awareness, CPR awareness, the duty to act, Good Samaritan principles, and what to document after a medical incident.

First Aid Basics

Security guards are not medical professionals; however, you are expected to take reasonable steps to assist. The exact steps depend on your training level, workplace procedures, and the situation. The most important rule is to **keep yourself safe** while helping others.

In many situations, your priorities are:

- Check for danger (for you and the injured person)
- Call for help early (911 or onsite medical response)
- Provide basic assistance within your training and comfort level

- Stay with the person until help arrives (if safe to do so)

Common examples of basic assistance include controlling minor bleeding, helping someone sit or lie safely, keeping them calm, and monitoring their condition. If the person is unconscious, having trouble breathing, or showing signs of a serious condition, call emergency services immediately.

A helpful mindset is: **do what you can safely, but do not exceed your training.**

CPR Awareness

CPR (Cardiopulmonary Resuscitation) is an emergency lifesaving technique used when a person is not breathing normally and may be in cardiac arrest. Not every guard is trained or certified in CPR, but you should understand the basics of what to do in an emergency.

If someone is unresponsive and not breathing normally, the most essential actions usually include:

1. Call 911 (or direct someone else to call)
2. Ask for an AED (Automated External Defibrillator) if one is available
3. Begin CPR if you are trained and it is safe to do so
4. Follow directions from emergency dispatchers and onsite procedures

If an AED is available, it should be used as soon as possible. AEDs are designed to give clear instructions and are commonly found in workplaces and public buildings.

Even if you cannot provide CPR, you can still help by calling for help, locating an AED, clearing space, and guiding responders to the scene.

Duty to Act

Duty to act refers to the responsibility to take reasonable steps to assist when you become aware of an emergency. In security work, this often means responding and adhering to workplace procedures. It does not mean that you must put yourself at risk or perform medical tasks for which you are not trained.

A security guard's duty to act typically includes:

- Taking the situation seriously
- Calling the right help early (911, onsite first aid, supervisor)
- Providing basic assistance with training and policy
- Staying calm and maintaining control of the area
- Documenting the incident properly afterward

If you ignore a medical emergency or delay calling for help, it can lead to serious consequences for the person and for you.

Good Samaritan Principles

Good Samaritan principles are meant to encourage people to help in emergencies without fear, as long as they act reasonably and in good faith. The key idea is that you should help within your abilities and not act recklessly.

For security guards, the safest approach is:

- Help in a reasonable way
- Follow site procedures
- Do not exceed your training
- Do not perform risky actions you are not qualified to do
- Get professional medical help as quickly as possible

On the exam, the correct answer is often the one that focuses on calling for help early, acting safely, and staying within your training.

Documentation After Incidents

Medical incidents must be documented clearly and respectfully. Good documentation supports the employer, helps identify hazards, and provides an accurate record if questions arise later.

Your report should focus on facts, such as:

- Date, time, and exact location
- What you observed (symptoms and behaviour)
- What actions did you take (whom you called, what help was provided)
- Names and roles of responders (first aid staff, paramedics, police, supervisor)
- Witness information if required by policy
- Outcome (transport to hospital, refusal of assistance, incident resolved)

Avoid adding opinions or medical diagnoses. For example, do not write "heart attack" unless a medical professional has confirmed it. Instead, write what you observed, such as "complained of chest pain and shortness of breath."

Also, remember confidentiality. Do not share medical details outside authorized reporting channels.

Chapter 8 Summary

You should now understand:

- Basic first aid response starts with safety, calling for help, and assisting within training
- CPR awareness includes recognizing emergencies, calling 911, and using

an AED if available

- Duty to act means taking reasonable steps to help and following the site procedure
- Good Samaritan principles support helping in good faith without reckless behaviour
- Medical incident documentation should be factual, objective, and respectful

* * *

Quick Check: Practice Questions (Chapter 8)

1) A person collapses and is not responding. What should happen first in most situations?

A. Immediately transport the person to a hospital in your vehicle
B. Call 911 (or have someone call) and follow emergency procedure
C. Leave the person alone to respect privacy
D. Wait to see if they recover on their own

2) Which statement best describes a security guard's duty to act in a medical emergency?

A. You must provide medical treatment even if untrained
B. You should ignore it unless a manager requests help
C. You must take reasonable steps, call for help, and follow procedure
D. You should only help if you know the person personally

3) Good Samaritan principles generally encourage people to:

A. Provide help in good faith and act reasonably within their abilities
B. Perform advanced medical procedures if they feel confident

C. Delay calling emergency services to avoid embarrassment

D. Diagnose the condition before offering assistance

4) Which is the best example of proper documentation after a medical incident?

A. "He had a heart attack. I saved him."

B. "She was probably faking it for attention."

C. "The person seemed drunk, so I ignored it."

D. "The person complained of chest pain and dizziness. 911 was called at 2:14 p.m. Paramedics arrived at 2:22 p.m."

Answers:

1) B

2) C

3) A

4) D

9

Health & Safety in the Workplace

Security guards work in many environments, and each presents hazards. You may work around vehicles, loading docks, chemicals, construction areas, slippery floors, aggressive behaviour, or poor lighting. Health and safety are not just "common sense." It is part of being professional and reducing risk for everyone on the site.

This chapter explains common workplace hazards, WHMIS basics, injury prevention, and how to report unsafe conditions.

Occupational Hazards

An occupational hazard is any work-related condition that can cause injury, illness, or harm. Some hazards are obvious, like an icy walkway. Others are less obvious, like stress, fatigue, or repeated lifting.

Common hazards security guards may face include:

- Slips, trips, and falls (wet floors, ice, clutter, uneven surfaces)
- Vehicles and equipment (forklifts, trucks, loading docks, parking lots)
- Environmental hazards (poor lighting, extreme cold/heat, noise)
- Workplace violence (aggressive customers, intoxication, domestic dis-

putes)
- Electrical hazards (exposed wiring, damaged outlets, unsafe cords)
- Biological hazards (blood or bodily fluids)
- Ergonomic hazards (long-standing, repetitive tasks, poor posture)

Your job is not to "fix" every hazard yourself. Your job is to recognize hazards early, take reasonable steps to reduce risk, and report them properly.

WHMIS Overview

WHMIS stands for **Workplace Hazardous Materials Information System**. It is Canada's system for communicating information about hazardous products used in workplaces. Many security guards will not handle chemicals directly, but you still need basic awareness because dangerous products may be present on site.

WHMIS helps workers understand:

- What a hazardous product is
- How to recognize hazard symbols and labels
- Where to find safety information (Safety Data Sheets, or SDS)
- How to handle and respond safely if exposed

You do not need to memorize every symbol for the licensing exam, but you should understand the purpose of WHMIS and what to do if you encounter a hazardous product incident.

If you see a chemical spill or strong fumes, do not rush in. Create distance, follow the site procedure, and call the appropriate help. Many chemical risks are not visible.

Preventing Injuries

Injury prevention is part of professionalism. It protects you, your coworkers, and the public. Many workplace injuries happen during routine tasks—walking quickly, lifting improperly, or ignoring small hazards.

Good injury prevention habits include:

- Stay alert during patrols and use proper footwear
- Walk, do not run, unless immediate safety requires it
- Use handrails and avoid carrying items that block your view
- Keep a safe distance from moving vehicles and equipment
- Avoid entering unsafe areas alone (especially at night)
- Use gloves or barriers if you must deal with bodily fluids, and follow the procedure
- Take breaks when possible and manage fatigue

Security guards often work long shifts. Fatigue leads to mistakes. A tired guard is more likely to miss hazards, misjudge situations, and get hurt.

Reporting Unsafe Conditions

Reporting hazards is a key part of safety culture. If you ignore a hazard, someone may get injured later. Reporting also protects you because it demonstrates that you recognized the risk and took action.

When reporting an unsafe condition, focus on facts:

- What the hazard is
- Where it is
- When you noticed it
- Who you notified
- What you did to reduce risk (if anything safe and appropriate)

Sometimes you can reduce risk immediately, such as placing a wet floor sign or blocking off a small area—if site policy allows it. But do not put yourself in danger. If the hazard is serious (e.g., chemical spill, exposed wires, structural issues), report and escalate immediately.

Chapter 9 Summary

You should now understand:

- Occupational hazards can be physical, environmental, chemical, biological, or behavioural
- WHMIS is Canada's hazard communication system for workplace hazardous products
- Preventing injuries depends on awareness, safe habits, and managing fatigue
- Reporting unsafe conditions is a professional responsibility and should be factual and timely

* * *

Quick Check: Practice Questions (Chapter 9)

1) Which statement best describes WHMIS?

A. A system for identifying and communicating hazards related to workplace hazardous materials

B. A police database used to track criminal suspects

C. A security guard licensing system used only in Ontario

D. A method for writing incident reports

2) You notice a chemical spill with a strong smell in a storage area. What is

the best initial action?

A. Clean it up immediately to prevent complaints

B. Create distance, follow the site procedure, and notify the appropriate people

C. Taste the substance to identify it

D. Ignore it if no one is nearby

3) Which is a common occupational hazard for security guards?

A. Only hazards related to theft

B. Only hazards related to fire alarms

C. Slips, trips, and falls during patrols

D. None, because security guards do not do physical work

4) What is the best example of reporting an unsafe condition?

A. "This place is unsafe. Someone should do something."

B. Posting a warning about the hazard on social media

C. Waiting until the end of the week to mention it casually

D. "At 7:10 p.m., I observed an icy patch at the north entrance. I placed a caution sign and notified the supervisor."

Answers:

1) A

2) B

3) C

4) D

IV

Communication & Interaction

Part 4 builds strong communication skills for security work. You'll learn how to speak professionally, use radio procedures, give clear directions, and manage conflict safely. This section focuses on de-escalation, respectful interaction with the public, cultural awareness, and choosing actions that reduce risk while following site procedures.

10

Communication Skills

Communication is one of the most important tools a security guard has. Most incidents can be prevented or reduced through calm, clear communication. Good communication helps you gain cooperation, reduce conflict, and keep situations safe without needing physical action.

Communication includes what you say, how you say it, and what your body language communicates. It also includes how you speak over the radio and how you represent your employer in public.

Verbal Communication

Verbal communication encompasses the words you use and how you deliver them. Security guards should speak clearly, calmly, and professionally—especially under stress. Your goal is to guide behaviour, not to argue.

Good verbal communication often includes:

- Speaking in a calm, steady tone
- Giving clear and straightforward instructions
- Using respectful words, even when others are rude
- Listening before responding

- Asking questions when you need more information
- Avoiding threats, sarcasm, or insults

A helpful method is to be direct but respectful. For example:

"Sir, this area is closed. Please step back behind the line."

If the person does not comply, do not escalate. Repeat the instruction calmly and explain what will happen next according to the procedure. For example:

"If you do not step back, I will need to call my supervisor."

Non-Verbal Communication

Non-verbal communication includes your posture, facial expression, gestures, tone, and distance from the person. In many situations, your body language will be noticed before your words.

Non-verbal communication can either calm a situation or make it worse. A professional guard aims for calm and control.

Examples of effective non-verbal communication include:

- Standing upright but relaxed
- Keeping hands visible and non-threatening
- Maintaining a safe distance
- Using neutral facial expressions
- Avoiding aggressive gestures, pointing, or crowding

A common mistake is standing too close or using a challenging posture. Even if your words are calm, your body language might communicate anger or threat.

Radio Procedures

Radio communication is a key skill in many security jobs. Good radio use keeps the team informed and helps supervisors and responders act quickly.

Radio messages should be:

- Clear and brief
- Professional
- Accurate
- Focused on what matters (who, what, where, and what help is needed)

Basic good practice includes:

- Think before you speak
- Identify who you are calling and who you are
- Use location details (not vague statements like "over here")
- Avoid personal opinions and jokes
- Avoid confidential information unless the procedure allows it

For example, instead of:

"Hey, come quick, there's a problem!"

A better message is:

"Control, this is Front Entrance. I have a disturbance at the main doors. Please send assistance."

Some sites use specific codes or plain language rules. Always follow the site procedure.

Professional Language

Professional language means speaking in a way that is respectful, neutral, and suitable for the workplace. This is important because your words can affect safety and can be used later in reports or complaints.

Professional language includes:

- Avoiding swearing, insults, or aggressive statements
- Avoiding racist, sexist, or discriminatory comments
- Avoiding threats (even if you are frustrated)
- Using simple, clear wording that reduces tension

The exam often tests professionalism through scenarios. If an answer choice contains insults, sarcasm, or threats, it is usually incorrect.

A good guard remains calm and neutral even when the other person is not.

Chapter 10 Summary

You should now understand:

- Verbal communication should be calm, clear, and respectful
- Non-verbal communication (posture, distance, gestures) affects how people respond
- Radio communication should be brief, accurate, and professional
- Professional language reduces conflict and protects you and your employer

* * *

Quick Check: Practice Questions (Chapter 10)

1) Which is an example of effective verbal communication by a security guard?

A. "If you don't leave right now, I'll make you leave."
B. "Please step back behind the line. This area is closed."
C. "What's wrong with you? Can't you read?"
D. "Do whatever you want. I don't care."

2) Which non-verbal behaviour is most likely to escalate a situation?

A. Standing too close and pointing aggressively
B. Keeping hands visible and posture relaxed
C. Maintaining a safe distance
D. Using a neutral facial expression

3) What is a key goal of professional radio communication?

A. To entertain the team and keep morale high
B. To share personal opinions about people on site
C. To provide clear, accurate information so the right help can respond
D. To avoid reporting problems unless asked

4) Which statement best reflects professional language?

A. "You're lucky I'm in a good mood today."
B. "I'm going to teach you a lesson."
C. "This is private property. You need to leave now, or I will call police."
D. "Move it, idiot."

Answers:

1) B

2) A
3) C
4) C

11

Conflict Management and De-escalation

Security guards often deal with conflict. It might be a customer who is angry, a visitor who refuses to follow rules, or a dispute between employees. In many cases, your goal is not to "win" the conversation. Your goal is to keep people safe and reduce the risk of violence.

De-escalation means using communication and behaviour to lower tension. It is one of the most important skills in security work because it prevents incidents from escalating into emergencies.

Stages of Conflict

Conflict usually develops in stages. Understanding these stages helps you respond early, before the situation becomes dangerous.

A simple way to think about conflict stages is:

- **Calm:** normal behaviour, no problem
- **Tension:** signs of frustration, raised voice, refusal to cooperate
- **Escalation:** threats, aggressive language, hostile posture
- **Crisis:** physical violence or immediate risk
- **Recovery:** emotions lower, situation becomes manageable

- **Post-incident:** reporting, follow-up, and prevention steps

The earlier you respond, the easier it is to control the situation. Waiting too long can turn a minor issue into a serious incident.

De-escalation Techniques

De-escalation is not about being weak. It is about being professional and safe. A calm guard is more likely to gain cooperation and less likely to trigger aggression.

Effective techniques include:

- **Stay calm:** keep a steady voice and controlled body language
- **Create space:** maintain a safe distance and an exit route
- **Listen:** let the person speak without interrupting
- **Show respect:** use polite language even if the person is rude
- **Use simple choices:** give clear options ("You can do X, or you will need to leave")
- **Set boundaries:** explain rules and consequences without threats
- **Call for backup early:** do not wait until the situation becomes unsafe

A helpful approach is to keep your instructions short and precise. Long speeches often increase tension.

Cultural Awareness

Ontario is diverse, and security guards interact with people from many backgrounds. Cultural awareness means recognizing that communication styles can differ. Eye contact, personal space, tone, gestures, and volume can mean different things to different people.

Cultural awareness does not mean changing the rules. It means applying rules fairly while communicating respectfully.

Good practice includes:

- Avoid assumptions about people based on appearance or accent
- Speak clearly, especially if English is a second language
- Be patient when someone is confused or stressed
- Treat everyone with the same level of respect and professionalism
- Focus on behaviour (what the person is doing), not personal identity

On the exam, answers that include stereotypes, insults, or discrimination are always incorrect.

Dealing with Aggressive Individuals

Aggression can include shouting, threats, intimidation, or violence. Your main goal is safety. Many aggressive situations can be managed without physical force if you stay calm and use safe tactics.

When dealing with an aggressive person:

- Maintain a safe distance and avoid cornering them
- Keep your hands visible and your posture non-threatening
- Use calm, clear commands
- Avoid arguing or matching their energy
- Watch for warning signs (clenched fists, pacing, sudden movements)
- Call for backup or police when needed
- If weapons are suspected, create distance and call the police immediately

If a person becomes violent or the risk is too high, your safest action may be to disengage and move to safety while calling for help.

Exam Focus: What to Say vs. What Not to Say

Many exam questions test your words. The correct answer is usually the one that is calm, respectful, and procedure-based.

What to say:

- Clear rules and directions: "This area is closed. Please step back."
- Calm choices: "You can leave voluntarily, or I will call the police."
- Respectful tone: "I understand you're upset. Let's talk calmly."

What not to say:

- Threats: "I'll make you leave."
- Insults: "You're acting stupid."
- Challenges: "Do you want to fight?"
- Personal comments: "People like you always cause trouble."

If an option sounds aggressive or insulting, it is almost never the correct answer.

Chapter 11 Summary

You should now understand:

- Conflict often develops in stages, and early response helps prevent escalation
- De-escalation uses calm communication, safe distance, and clear boundaries
- Cultural awareness helps you communicate respectfully without bias
- Aggressive situations require safety-first decisions and early backup when needed
- Exam questions often test what a guard should say and what a guard

should avoid saying

* * *

Quick Check: Practice Questions (Chapter 11)

1) Which response is the best example of de-escalation language?

A. "Calm down right now, or else."
B. "You're being ridiculous. Leave."
C. "I understand you're upset. Let's talk calmly and figure this out."
D. "Say that again and see what happens."

2) Which is a sign that a conflict may be escalating?

A. A person asks a question politely
B. A person clenches fists, raises voice, and moves closer
C. A person follows instructions and leaves the area
D. A person thanks you for your help

3) Cultural awareness in security work means:

A. Enforcing rules differently for different groups
B. Ignoring site rules to avoid complaints
C. Making assumptions based on accent or appearance
D. Applying rules fairly while communicating respectfully and without bias

4) A person becomes aggressive and you suspect they may have a weapon. What is the safest action?

A. Move closer to control them quickly
B. Challenge them to show authority

C. Create distance, move to safety, and call police immediately

D. Continue arguing until they calm down

Answers:

1) C

2) B

3) D

4) C

V

REPORT WRITING

Part 5 teaches report writing for security work. You'll learn how to write clear, factual, and professional notes that can be used by supervisors, clients, and police. This section covers what to include, what to avoid, common mistakes, and how to write incident reports with accurate timelines, observations, and actions taken.

12

Report Writing Fundamentals

Report writing is one of the most important skills for a security guard. A report creates a written record of what happened, what you observed, and what actions you took. Reports may be read by supervisors, clients, police, insurers, or lawyers. A clear report can protect the public, your employer, and you.

A good report is not about writing "perfect English." It is about writing **clear facts** in a way that another person can understand.

Why Reports Matter

Reports matter because they:

- Create an official record of incidents and actions taken
- Help supervisors and clients understand risks and trends
- Support police investigations when needed
- Help resolve complaints or disputes
- Protect you by showing you acted reasonably and followed procedure

In many cases, your report may be the only written evidence of an incident. If it is unclear, contains missing details, or is overly opinionated, it can cause problems later.

Types of Reports

Security guards may write different kinds of reports depending on the site and employer. The names may vary, but common types include:

- **Daily activity reports (DAR):** a summary of routine duties during the shift
- **Incident reports:** detailed reports about specific events (theft, injury, disturbance, alarm)
- **Occurrence reports:** another common term for incident reports
- **Shift logs or logbook entries:** brief notes of important events and times
- **Witness statements:** sometimes collected by supervisors or police, not always by guards

Some sites require reports for every unusual event, even if it seems minor. When in doubt, follow post orders and ask your supervisor.

What Makes a Report Legally Sound

A legally sound report is factual, clear, and reliable. It should show what happened and what you did, without exaggeration or emotion.

A strong report usually includes:

- **Date, time, and location** (be specific)
- **Who was involved** (names if known, descriptions if not)
- **What you observed** (what you saw and heard)
- **Actions taken** (who you contacted, what steps you took)
- **Witnesses** (names/contact details if policy allows)
- **Outcome** (police called, person left, ambulance arrived, etc.)

A key exam idea is that good reports include a clear timeline. If you can't remember the time, do not guess. Use your notes, radio logs, or site systems if available.

Also, never alter reports to protect someone or avoid trouble. Honesty is critical.

Objectivity vs. Opinion

Objectivity means sticking to facts that you observed. Opinion is a personal belief or assumption. Security reports should be objective.

Objective statements describe what happened:
"The individual was shouting and using profanity."
"The individual refused to leave after being asked twice."
"I observed the person place two items into a backpack."

Opinion statements guess motives or feelings:
"He was drunk and looking for trouble."
"She was lying."
"He stole the items because he is a criminal."

Unless you are a qualified professional, you should not diagnose or label. Instead, describe what you saw. If you suspect intoxication, write observable signs:

"Smell of alcohol on breath, slurred speech, unsteady walking."

This is a common exam focus. If a question asks which report sentence is best, the correct answer is usually the one that contains observable facts, not personal judgment.

Chapter 12 Summary

You should now understand:

- Reports matter because they create an official record and can be used by supervisors, clients, police, and others
- Security guards write different types of reports depending on the site and employer
- Legally sound reports are clear, factual, complete, and include a timeline and actions taken
- Objective reporting focuses on what you observed, not your opinions or assumptions

* * *

Quick Check: Practice Questions (Chapter 12)

1) Why do security reports matter?

A. They help create an official record and may be used in investigations or disputes

B. They are only for entertainment and training

C. They replace the need for calling police

D. They are optional if you remember what happened

2) Which sentence is the best example of objective reporting?

A. "He was obviously guilty and lying."

B. "She is a troublemaker and always causes problems."

C. "The person smelled of alcohol, slurred speech, and staggered while walking."

D. "He looked like a criminal."

3) Which item helps make a report legally sound?

A. Personal opinions about the person involved

B. A clear timeline and factual description of actions taken

C. Humour to make the report easier to read

D. Removing details to avoid complaints

4) Which is an example of an incident report (occurrence report)?

A. A short summary of routine patrols with no unusual events

B. A personal diary entry about how your shift felt

C. A detailed report describing a theft, who was involved, and what actions were taken

D. A note written days later based on memory alone

Answers:

1) A

2) C

3) B

4) C

13

Writing an Effective Incident Report

An incident report (sometimes called an occurrence report) is used when something unusual happens on site. The purpose is to create a clear, factual record that another person can understand without needing you to explain it later. A well-written report is calm, organized, and detailed enough to answer basic questions.

A good incident report should read like a professional summary of events, not a story, argument, or personal opinion.

The "5 Ws": Who, What, When, Where, Why

Most strong incident reports can be checked using the "5 Ws." If you include these, your report will usually be complete.

Who

- Who was involved? (names if known, otherwise descriptions)
- Who witnessed the event?
- Who did you notify? (supervisor, client contact, police, EMS)

What

- What happened?
- What did you observe directly?
- What actions did you take?

When

- Date and times (start time, key events, time police/EMS arrived, time resolved)

Where

- Exact location (building, floor, room, entrance, parking lot section)

Why

- Why did you take specific actions (based on safety and procedure)
- If you don't know why something happened, do not guess. State what you know.

Many reports fail because they are missing times, locations, or clear actions taken.

Common Report-Writing Errors

Most report-writing errors fall into a few patterns. Avoid these, and your report quality improves immediately.

1) Opinions and assumptions

"He was lying."
"She was drunk."
"He did it on purpose."

Instead, write what you observed.

2) Missing timeline

"Later, the police came."

Instead, include times when possible.

3) Unclear writing

"They got mad, and things happened."

Instead, describe the actual actions and words.

4) Too much emotion

"I couldn't believe how rude he was!"

Reports should stay calm and neutral.

5) Using slang or jokes

Reports are formal documents. Keep language professional.

6) Leaving out your actions

Your report should show what you did and why, especially if you called the police or gave instructions.

7) Guessing

If you are not sure, do not guess. Use "I observed..." or "I was advised..." and identify the source.

Sample Incident Report (Annotated)

Below is a sample report with notes showing what makes it strong. You can copy this format and adjust it to your site requirements.

Sample Report

Date: May 14, 2026
Time: 19:05 hours
Location: Main Entrance, 123 Example Street, City, ON
Reporting Guard: M. Smith, Security Guard

Incident Type: Disturbance / Refusal to Leave

Narrative:
At approximately 19:05 hours, I observed an adult male standing inside the main entrance doors near the reception desk. The male was yelling and using profanity toward the reception staff. The male was approximately 5'10", medium build, wearing a black jacket and blue jeans. I approached and maintained a safe distance of approximately 2 metres.

I identified myself as security and stated, "Sir, please lower your voice. How can I help you?" The male said, "They won't help me. I'm not leaving." I advised the male that shouting and profanity were not permitted in the lobby and asked him to speak calmly or leave the property. The male continued yelling and refused to leave.

At 19:08 hours, I contacted Control by radio and requested a supervisor attend the main entrance. At 19:10 hours, the male stepped closer toward the reception staff while continuing to yell. I repositioned myself between the male and the reception, maintaining distance and keeping my hands visible. I again directed the male to leave the property. The male refused.

At 19:12 hours, I contacted the police via 911 due to continued aggressive behaviour and refusal to leave after multiple requests. At 19:18 hours, police arrived at the main entrance. I provided the police with a summary of events and the male's description. Police spoke with the male and escorted him out of the building at 19:23 hours. The male left without further incident.

No injuries were observed or reported. Reception staff were advised to contact their manager for follow-up. I completed this report at 19:40 hours.

End of Report

What This Report Does Well (Annotations)

- It includes a clear **timeline** with multiple time points.
- It uses **observable facts** ("yelling," "using profanity," "stepped closer") rather than opinions.
- It documents **actions taken** and **why** (calling the police due to refusal to leave and aggression).
- It describes the subject in case identification is needed later.
- It avoids medical or legal conclusions and stays neutral.

Chapter 13 Summary

You should now understand:

- Strong incident reports answer who, what, when, where, and why
- Common mistakes include opinions, missing timelines, vague writing, and guessing
- A good report is factual, clear, and includes your actions and outcomes
- Exam questions usually reward facts-only writing with accurate details

Quick Check: Practice Questions (Chapter 13)

1) Which sentence is best for an incident report?

A. "He was a criminal and definitely stole it."

B. "The person was acting crazy and being a jerk."

C. "I observed the person place two items into a backpack and walk past the cash registers without paying."

D. "Everyone knows she lies all the time."

2) What is one of the most common report-writing errors?

A. Including exact times and locations

B. Writing in a calm, neutral tone

C. Explaining what actions you took

D. Adding opinions and assumptions instead of observations

3) The "5 Ws" help make sure your report includes:

A. Who, what, when, where, and why

B. Who, which, while, where, and whether

C. When, where, which, why, and would

D. What, where, who, whom, and whose

4) If you are unsure about a detail (for example, a time), the best approach is to:

A. Guess so the report sounds complete

B. Leave the report blank and do not submit it

C. Write "I am sure it was around..." and pick a time

D. Use notes or system records if available, and only state what you can support

Answers:

1) C
2) D
3) A
4) D

VI

CANADIAN LEGAL SYSTEM

Part 6 explains the basics of Canada's legal system and how it relates to security work. You'll learn the difference between criminal and civil law, the structure of courts in Ontario, and the roles of police, courts, and corrections. This section helps you understand legal terms used on the exam and why proper procedure and documentation matter.

14

Canadian Legal Foundations

Security guards do not need to be legal experts, but you do need basic legal knowledge to work safely and professionally. The Ontario licensing exam includes legal terms and concepts that help you understand your role, your limits, and how security work connects to the justice system.

This chapter explains the differences between criminal and civil law, the basic court structure in Ontario, the roles of the police, courts, and corrections, and how security work fits within the broader system.

Criminal Law vs. Civil Law

Canadian law is often grouped into **criminal law** and **civil law**. They are different in purpose, process, and outcomes.

Criminal law deals with offences against the public and society. Examples include assault, theft, and mischief. Criminal cases are usually investigated by police and prosecuted by the government (the Crown). The outcome may consist of fines, probation, or imprisonment.

Civil law deals with disputes between individuals or organizations. Examples include lawsuits for injuries, property damage, or breach of contract. Civil cases are about compensation or legal remedies, not punishment.

A simple way to remember the difference is:

- Criminal law = the state vs. a person (public offences)
- Civil law = one person/organization vs. another (private disputes)

Security guards may be involved in both types. For example, a theft incident may result in criminal charges, whereas an injury during the incident may give rise to a civil lawsuit.

Court Structure in Ontario

You do not need to memorize every court level, but you should understand the general structure and the idea that different courts handle different matters.

In Ontario, courts commonly include:

- **Ontario Court of Justice:** handles many criminal matters and provincial offences, as well as some family matters
- **Superior Court of Justice:** handles more serious criminal matters, major civil cases, and other important legal issues
- **Court of Appeal for Ontario:** reviews decisions from lower courts when appealed

The key examination idea is that the court system has tiers, and serious matters may be appealed to higher courts. Security guards are most likely to be involved as witnesses, providing reports or testimony.

Roles of Police, Courts, and Corrections

The justice system has different parts that work together.

Police
Police investigate crimes, collect evidence, and enforce criminal law. They may arrest and lay charges where appropriate.

Courts
Courts decide whether a person is guilty or not guilty, based on evidence and legal rules. Courts also decide penalties and other legal outcomes.

Corrections
Corrections manages people who are serving sentences. This can include custody (jail/prison), probation, parole supervision, and rehabilitation programs.

Security guards are not part of the police or corrections. Your role is to prevent problems where possible and to respond professionally when incidents occur. Your actions and reports can still be important in a criminal case or civil case.

How Security Work Fits into the Justice System

Security guards support public safety, but they do it through private employment and site authority. Security is often the first line of prevention. A professional guard may:

- Deter offences through presence and access control
- Observe and report incidents accurately
- Protect evidence by documenting facts and preserving information (like video)
- Contact the police when criminal matters occur
- Provide statements and testify if needed

This is why professional behaviour and report writing matter so much. In many cases, your report becomes part of the evidence used to make decisions later.

A guard's best contribution is usually not physical intervention—it is **calm decision-making, accurate observations, and clear documentation**.

Chapter 14 Summary

You should now understand:

- Criminal law involves offences against society and is prosecuted by the government
- Civil law involves disputes between people or organizations and often focuses on compensation
- Ontario's court system has levels, including the Ontario Court of Justice and the Superior Court of Justice
- Police investigate and enforce, courts decide outcomes, and corrections manage sentences
- Security guards support the justice system through prevention, observation, reporting, and proper escalation

Quick Check: Practice Questions (Chapter 14)

1) Which statement best describes criminal law?

A. Disputes between two private companies about a contract
B. Offences against society that are prosecuted by the government
C. A complaint about poor customer service
D. A disagreement between neighbours over noise

2) A person sues a business for injuries after slipping on a wet floor. This is most likely:

A. Civil law

B. Criminal law

C. A provincial offence case only

D. A corrections matter

3) Which group is mainly responsible for deciding guilt or innocence in criminal cases?

A. Corrections

B. Security guards

C. Courts

D. Insurance companies

4) How does security work most often fit into the justice system?

A. By replacing police investigations

B. By laying criminal charges directly

C. By sentencing offenders

D. By deterring incidents, observing, reporting, and contacting police when needed

Answers:

1) B

2) A

3) C

4) D

VII

PRACTICE EXAMS

15

Practice Exam #1

Instructions: Choose the **best** answer for each question (A, B, C, or D). Read carefully. Many questions are scenario-based and test what a professional guard should do first.

Questions 1–60

1) The main purpose of a security guard is to:

A. Investigate crimes and lay charges
B. Replace police on private property
C. Search and detain anyone suspected of theft
D. Deter, observe, report, and assist

2) Which action best shows professionalism?

A. Posting incident details online to warn others
B. Using insulting language to gain control
C. Staying calm and following site procedure
D. Ignoring visitors who ask for help

3) A conflict of interest is most likely when a guard:

A. Accepts a gift to ignore a rule violation

B. Writes a clear incident report
C. Calls police during a disturbance
D. Checks doors during patrol

4) Under PSISA, a security guard should:
A. Present themselves as police to gain cooperation
B. Follow the Code of Conduct and act professionally
C. Ignore site post orders if they disagree
D. Work without a licence if supervised

5) A guard's authority on a site mainly comes from:
A. Police powers while on duty
B. Court orders given to security guards
C. Being a private citizen and an agent of the property owner/employer
D. The ability to issue fines

6) Which situation is most appropriate for calling police immediately?
A. A visitor asks for directions
B. A person refuses to sign in but leaves when asked
C. A customer complains about parking rules
D. A suspected weapon is seen during a disturbance

7) Which statement about a citizen's arrest is most accurate?
A. Security guards may arrest anyone who breaks a site rule
B. Security guards have broader arrest powers than police
C. Citizen's arrest powers are limited and must meet legal conditions
D. A guard can arrest only if the person admits guilt

8) A guard should NOT arrest when:
A. They directly witness an offence and it is safe to act
B. They have only suspicion and did not observe the offence
C. Police request assistance and it is safe
D. The person is actively damaging property and safety is at risk

9) "Reasonable force" means:

A. Any amount of force needed to make someone obey

B. Force used to punish someone for misconduct

C. The least force necessary and appropriate for the situation

D. Force that continues until the person apologizes

10) Which is an example of excessive force?

A. Creating distance and calling for help

B. Using minimal force to protect someone from immediate harm

C. Continuing force after the person is controlled and no longer a threat

D. Speaking calmly and giving clear directions

11) Situational assessment includes thinking about:

A. Threat level, environment, and availability of backup

B. Whether the person "deserves" consequences

C. How to win the argument

D. How to avoid writing a report

12) A consent search means:

A. The guard searches whenever they want on private property

B. The person voluntarily agrees to be searched

C. The guard can force the search if the person refuses

D. The guard must detain the person first

13) A person refuses a bag check required for entry. The best response is to:

A. Search the bag anyway

B. Allow entry but note it in the log

C. Deny entry and follow site procedure

D. Confiscate the bag

14) Detention means:

A. Asking someone to wait (they can refuse)

B. Writing down someone's name

C. Keeping someone from leaving when they are not free to go
D. Talking to someone on camera

15) Which action is most appropriate with a suspicious package?
A. Move it to a safer location
B. Open it carefully to check contents
C. Throw it outside immediately
D. Do not touch it; create distance and follow procedure

16) During a fire alarm, a guard should generally:
A. Assume it is false until smoke is seen
B. Support evacuation and follow the site emergency plan
C. Lock exits to prevent theft
D. Use elevators to speed evacuation

17) If a bomb threat is received by phone, the guard should:
A. Argue with the caller to show confidence
B. Hang up immediately without listening
C. Stay calm, gather details, then notify according to procedure
D. Announce the threat to everyone before notifying anyone

18) "Lockdown" is usually used when:
A. It is safer to keep people inside secured areas than to evacuate
B. The building is closed for cleaning
C. There is a minor dispute at reception
D. The fire alarm has ended

19) In a medical emergency, the best first step is usually to:
A. Diagnose the condition before doing anything
B. Call 911 (or have someone call) and follow procedure
C. Leave for privacy reasons
D. Wait to see if the person improves

20) Which statement best reflects duty to act?

A. Ignore emergencies unless asked by a manager
B. Take reasonable steps, call for help, and follow site procedure
C. Provide advanced medical treatment even if untrained
D. Avoid reporting medical incidents to protect confidentiality

21) Good Samaritan principles generally support:

A. Helping in good faith and acting reasonably within your abilities
B. Performing medical procedures you are not trained to do
C. Delaying calls to emergency services
D. Sharing medical details with coworkers

22) The best example of objective medical documentation is:

A. "He was faking it."
B. "She had a heart attack. I saved her."
C. "The person complained of chest pain; 911 was called at 2:14 p.m."
D. "He was drunk and caused problems."

23) WHMIS is mainly about:

A. Radio communication rules
B. Hazardous product information in workplaces
C. Criminal investigations
D. Court procedures

24) You notice a strong chemical smell and a spill in a storage area. You should:

A. Clean it up immediately
B. Taste it to identify it
C. Create distance, notify, and follow site procedure
D. Ignore it if no one is nearby

25) A common hazard for security guards is:

A. Only theft-related risk

B. Slips, trips, and falls during patrols

C. No hazards because guards don't do physical work

D. Hazards only during emergencies

26) Reporting an unsafe condition should include:

A. Only your opinion about who is to blame

B. Facts: what, where, when, who you notified, and actions taken

C. A social media post for awareness

D. Waiting until the end of the week

27) Effective verbal communication usually includes:

A. Threats to gain control quickly

B. Clear, calm, respectful instructions

C. Sarcasm to show authority

D. Matching the person's anger to dominate the situation

28) Non-verbal communication that may escalate conflict includes:

A. Keeping a safe distance

B. Hands visible and calm posture

C. Standing too close and pointing aggressively

D. Neutral facial expression

29) A professional radio message should be:

A. Long and detailed with opinions

B. Vague to avoid responsibility

C. Full of jokes to keep morale up

D. Clear, brief, and accurate

30) Which statement is most professional?

A. "Move it, idiot."

B. "You're lucky I'm in a good mood."

C. "This area is restricted. Please step back."

D. "Do what you want. I don't care."

31) Conflict is easier to manage when a guard:

A. Waits until the person becomes violent

B. Responds early during the tension stage

C. Uses force to end it quickly

D. Insults the person to "shock" them into compliance

32) A good de-escalation technique is to:

A. Argue until the person admits they are wrong

B. Crowd the person to show control

C. Use calm tone, listen, and give simple choices

D. Threaten arrest to force cooperation

33) Cultural awareness means:

A. Enforcing rules differently for different people

B. Applying rules fairly while communicating respectfully

C. Making assumptions based on accent or appearance

D. Ignoring conflict to avoid complaints

34) If you suspect a person may have a weapon, you should:

A. Move closer to control them quickly

B. Create distance and call police immediately

C. Challenge them to show authority

D. Continue arguing until they calm down

35) The main reason reports matter is that they:

A. Are optional and only for internal use

B. Create a record that may be used later by others

C. Replace the need to call police

D. Are used mainly to punish staff

36) A daily activity report (DAR) is usually:

A. A summary of routine activities during a shift

B. A court document written by police

C. A medical chart for injuries
D. A confidential personal diary

37) A legally sound report should include:
A. Opinions about the subject's character
B. A clear timeline, location, observations, and actions taken
C. Jokes to make it easier to read
D. Only one sentence to keep it short

38) Which sentence is the most objective?
A. "He looked guilty."
B. "She is always causing trouble."
C. "I observed the person shouting and using profanity."
D. "He was lying to me."

39) The "5 Ws" are used to ensure a report includes:
A. Who, what, when, where, and why
B. What, when, which, where, and would
C. Who, which, whom, whose, and why
D. When, where, while, what, and whether

40) A common report-writing error is:
A. Writing facts and actions taken
B. Including times and locations
C. Guessing and adding assumptions
D. Using clear, simple language

41) If you are unsure about a detail, you should:
A. Guess so the report sounds complete
B. Leave it out and deny it happened
C. Use notes or system records and state only what you can support
D. Change the detail later if someone complains

42) Criminal law generally deals with:

A. Disputes between neighbours about noise
B. Private contract disagreements
C. Offences against society prosecuted by the government
D. Workplace scheduling problems

43) Civil law is most often about:

A. Punishing offenders with jail time
B. Disputes between individuals/organizations, often about compensation
C. Police investigations
D. Licensing exams

44) In criminal cases, courts mainly:

A. Decide guilt or innocence based on evidence and law
B. Patrol buildings and respond to alarms
C. Write security reports
D. Manage probation directly

45) Police are mainly responsible for:

A. Sentencing offenders
B. Investigating crimes and enforcing criminal law
C. Running private security companies
D. Approving security guard uniforms

46) Corrections is mainly responsible for:

A. Preventing theft in stores
B. Court decisions on guilt or innocence
C. Licensing security guards
D. Managing people serving sentences and supervision programs

47) Security work fits into the justice system mainly by:

A. Replacing police investigations
B. Laying criminal charges directly

C. Preventing incidents, observing, reporting, and contacting police when needed

D. Deciding court outcomes

48) A guard should keep reports confidential because:

A. Reports are gossip and not serious documents

B. Reports contain sensitive information and should be shared only with authorized people

C. Reports should be posted online for transparency

D. Reports are not used by anyone else

49) A guard finds a person sleeping in a restricted area. The person leaves peacefully when asked. The best action is to:

A. Arrest them for trespassing automatically

B. Write a brief report/log entry and notify as required

C. Use force to ensure they don't return

D. Ignore it completely

50) A guard sees two people arguing loudly in a lobby. The best first step is usually to:

A. Join the argument to show authority

B. Use calm verbal commands and create space

C. Push them apart immediately

D. Wait until someone gets hit

51) Which phrase is most likely to de-escalate?

A. "Do you want to fight?"

B. "You people always do this."

C. "I understand you're upset. Let's talk calmly."

D. "Say that again and see what happens."

52) A person refuses to give ID when asked. The best general response is to:

A. Force them to give ID

B. Explain the request and follow procedure if they refuse
C. Arrest them for refusing ID
D. Search them for identification

53) A guard sees a slip hazard (wet floor) near an entrance. A professional action is to:

A. Ignore it because it's not security-related
B. Put up a caution sign if allowed and report it
C. Blame housekeeping in a report
D. Block the exit permanently

54) A guard hears an alarm and sees smoke near a doorway. The guard should:

A. Investigate alone without notifying anyone
B. Activate/confirm emergency response per procedure and call for help
C. Assume it's a drill and continue patrol
D. Post online asking if anyone knows what's happening

55) A guard is writing an incident report. Which is best practice?

A. Use opinions so the reader knows how you felt
B. Write facts, actions taken, times, and outcomes
C. Leave out details to avoid complaints
D. Write it days later from memory only

56) Which is the best example of professional radio use?

A. "Hey, it's crazy over here, come now!"
B. "Control, I need help." (no location)
C. "Control, this is Parking Lot Patrol. Disturbance near south entrance. Request assistance."
D. "You won't believe what this guy just said..."

57) A person is shouting and moving closer to staff. The guard should:

A. Keep safe distance, set boundaries, and call for backup early

B. Insult the person to take control

C. Challenge them to prove confidence

D. Grab them immediately to end it

58) Which situation is most likely civil, not criminal?

A. Assault in a parking lot

B. Theft from a store

C. A customer sues after being injured in a fall

D. Mischief (property damage)

59) A guard is asked by a friend to "let them in" without signing in. The best response is to:

A. Let them in because you know them

B. Follow normal access procedure or contact a supervisor

C. Ignore the request and walk away

D. Sign them in yourself using a fake name

60) The best overall approach to emergencies is to:

A. Take control by acting alone and quickly

B. Focus on protecting property first

C. Prioritize personal/life safety, call help early, follow procedure, then document

D. Wait for a supervisor before doing anything

16

Practice Exam #2

Instructions: Choose the **best** answer for each question (A, B, C, or D). Questions are based on Ontario security guard training topics and common exam-style scenarios.

1) Which statement best describes the role of a security guard?

A. To investigate crimes and lay charges
B. To deter problems, observe, report, and assist
C. To act as police on private property
D. To search anyone suspected of theft

2) A professional guard should primarily focus on:

A. Winning arguments with difficult people
B. Safety, procedure, and calm communication
C. Punishing rule-breakers
D. Avoiding all interaction with the public

3) Under PSISA expectations, which behaviour is most appropriate?

A. Using threats to gain cooperation
B. Acting as if you are police
C. Acting honestly and with professionalism
D. Ignoring post orders when you disagree

4) Which is the clearest example of unethical behaviour?

A. Writing a factual report

B. Calling police when required

C. Accepting money to "look the other way"

D. Asking a visitor to leave calmly

5) To work legally as a security guard in Ontario, you generally must:

A. Hold a valid security guard licence

B. Be supervised by a manager at all times

C. Wear a uniform at every site

D. Have previous police or military experience

6) If your site requires guards to carry identification while working, the best practice is to:

A. Carry your licence/ID as required and present it when appropriate

B. Leave it in your car to avoid losing it

C. Only show it if the public demands it

D. Never show it to anyone under any circumstances

7) Which action is most clearly prohibited as a general professional standard?

A. Writing an objective incident report

B. Calling police when safety requires it

C. Enforcing site rules fairly

D. Presenting yourself in a way that makes people think you are police

8) A security guard's arrest power is best described as:

A. Limited powers similar to a private citizen (citizen's arrest)

B. The same powers as police while on duty

C. The power to arrest anyone who breaks site rules

D. The power to arrest only with supervisor approval

9) Section 494 of the Criminal Code is commonly connected to:

A. Citizen's arrest authority
B. WHMIS requirements
C. Fire code inspections
D. Civil lawsuits

10) After a lawful arrest, the best general next step is to:
A. Contact police as soon as possible and follow site procedure
B. Question the person until they confess
C. Search the person automatically for evidence
D. Delay reporting until the shift ends

11) "Reasonable force" is best described as:
A. Whatever force ends the situation fastest
B. The least force necessary and appropriate for the circumstances
C. Force used to punish misconduct
D. Force used whenever someone refuses directions

12) Proportionality means:
A. Force should always be physical if someone is rude
B. Force should continue until the person apologizes
C. The response should match the level of threat
D. The response should be the same in every incident

13) Which is an example of excessive force?
A. Maintaining distance and using calm verbal direction
B. Continuing to use force after the person is controlled and no longer a threat
C. Calling for backup early
D. Redirecting foot traffic for safety

14) The main purpose of a use-of-force continuum is to:
A. Help choose the least forceful effective response for the situation
B. Encourage guards to "move up" quickly to gain control

C. Replace post orders and site policy
D. Justify force whenever someone is uncooperative

15) Situational assessment includes:
A. Threat level, environment, weapons risk, and availability of backup
B. Deciding who is "right" in an argument
C. Planning how to avoid writing a report
D. Choosing the toughest response to show authority

16) A consent search is best described as a search that:
A. Happens automatically on private property
B. Happens only if police are present
C. Occurs when the person voluntarily agrees
D. Occurs after you detain the person

17) A person says, "I don't want to be searched." The most professional response is to:
A. Explain the policy and follow the procedure if they refuse (for example, deny entry)
B. Search anyway because it is private property
C. Detain them until they agree
D. Confiscate their property at the desk

18) Which statement about "seizing" property is most accurate for most guard roles?
A. Guards can seize any item they suspect is stolen
B. Guards should follow procedure and involve police when appropriate; seizure powers are limited
C. Guards should keep suspected stolen items as punishment
D. Guards should take items first and ask questions later

19) You discover a suspicious package in an unusual location. The best first action is to:

A. Keep people away and create distance, then follow procedure
B. Open it carefully to check
C. Move it outside
D. Shake it to listen for sounds

20) A bomb threat is received by phone. The best approach is to:

A. Hang up immediately
B. Argue with the caller
C. Stay calm, gather details if possible, then notify as required
D. Broadcast the threat over the radio to everyone

21) During a fire alarm, a guard should generally:

A. Assume it's false unless flames are visible
B. Support evacuation and follow the site emergency plan
C. Block exits to prevent theft
D. Use elevators to speed evacuation

22) A lockdown is generally used when:

A. The building needs cleaning
B. A minor argument occurs at reception
C. It is safer to keep people secured inside than to evacuate
D. A fire alarm has ended

23) A person collapses and is unresponsive. Your best first step is usually to:

A. Call 911 (or have someone call) and follow emergency procedure
B. Look for their ID before doing anything
C. Move them to another room for privacy
D. Wait to see if they wake up

24) If an AED is available during a suspected cardiac arrest, the best action is to:

A. Avoid using it unless a doctor is present

B. Hide it to prevent liability

C. Use it only after the person regains consciousness

D. Bring it immediately and follow its prompts (and your training/procedure)

25) Duty of care in security work most closely means:

A. You must physically intervene in every incident

B. You should ignore hazards unless someone complains

C. You should avoid calling police to protect the client's image

D. You must act reasonably to prevent harm and follow procedure

26) WHMIS is primarily about:

A. Criminal law procedures

B. Radio codes used by police

C. Communicating hazards of workplace products (labels/SDS)

D. Court structure in Ontario

27) When reporting an unsafe condition, the best approach is to:

A. Only report it if someone is injured

B. Report facts (what/where/when) and notify the right person promptly

C. Wait until the end of the week

D. Post a warning online

28) Which is a good injury-prevention habit for guards?

A. Running during patrols to save time

B. Standing in blind corners to "catch" people

C. Using safe footwear, staying alert, and avoiding unnecessary risks

D. Carrying heavy items that block your view

29) A professional radio message should include:

A. Who you are, where you are, what's happening, and what you need

B. Jokes to keep morale up

C. Personal opinions about the subject

D. Slang and insults to show authority

30) Which phrase is the most professional?

A. "Move it, idiot."
B. "This area is restricted. Please step back."
C. "Do what you want—I don't care."
D. "You're lucky I'm in a good mood."

31) Which statement is best for de-escalation?

A. "Say that again and see what happens."
B. "You people are always causing problems."
C. "Calm down right now, or else."
D. "I can see you're upset. Let's talk calmly and work this out."

32) Which example best matches the tension stage of conflict?

A. Normal conversation and cooperation
B. Physical violence has started
C. The incident is over and emotions are lowering
D. Raised voice, frustration, and refusal to cooperate

33) Cultural awareness in security work means:

A. Enforcing rules differently for different groups
B. Ignoring site rules to avoid complaints
C. Applying rules fairly while communicating respectfully and without bias
D. Asking people about their background to decide how to respond

34) If someone becomes aggressive and is moving toward staff, a guard should generally:

A. Keep distance, set boundaries, call for backup early, and prioritize safety
B. Crowd the person to show control
C. Challenge them to prove confidence
D. Grab them immediately to end it

35) Which sentence is best for an incident report?

A. "He's a troublemaker and probably guilty."

B. "She was lying and deserved it."

C. "He looked like a criminal."

D. "I observed the person shout and strike the counter with a closed fist."

36) What are the "5 Ws" in report writing?

A. Where, whenever, while, which, would

B. Who, which, whom, whose, why

C. What, when, whichever, where, whether

D. Who, what, when, where, why

37) Which is a common report-writing error?

A. Using clear times and locations

B. Writing in plain language

C. Describing actions taken

D. Guessing motives and adding assumptions

38) A legally sound report is one that is:

A. Factual, clear, and based on what you observed (with timeline and actions)

B. Written like a story to make it interesting

C. Short enough to avoid details

D. Focused on opinions so the reader knows your feelings

39) Criminal law usually deals with:

A. Offences against society prosecuted by the government

B. Customer service complaints

C. Workplace scheduling disputes

D. Private contract disagreements

40) Which group is primarily responsible for deciding guilt or innocence in criminal matters?

A. Security guards

B. Courts

C. Corrections

D. Insurance companies

41) Security work fits into the justice system mainly by:

A. Sentencing offenders

B. Replacing police investigations

C. Laying charges directly in court

D. Deterring incidents, observing, reporting, and contacting police when needed

42) Why should reports be kept confidential?

A. Reports are not serious documents

B. Reports may contain sensitive information and should be shared only with authorized people

C. Reports should be posted online for transparency

D. Reports are only for entertainment

43) A customer says, "That person stole earlier today," but you did not see it and have no evidence. The best action is usually to:

A. Arrest immediately based on the statement

B. Search the person without consent

C. Observe, gather facts, notify a supervisor, and call police if appropriate

D. Use force to stop the person from leaving

44) A person refuses to leave private property after being told they are not allowed there. The best general approach is to:

A. Fight them to prove authority

B. Ignore them to avoid conflict

C. Confiscate their phone until they leave

D. Follow procedure, keep safe distance, and involve police if required

45) In an active threat situation, the best priority for most guards is:

A. Chasing the threat alone

B. Taking control by physically engaging

C. Personal/life safety, warning others, and calling police early

D. Continuing normal duties to avoid panic

46) Which action best supports safety when dealing with workplace violence risk?

A. Waiting until a person becomes violent before calling for help

B. Calling for backup early and maintaining safe distance

C. Using insults to "shock" the person into compliance

D. Cornering the person to prevent movement

47) Which is good evidence-handling practice?

A. Handling items repeatedly to inspect them

B. Posting photos of evidence online

C. Throwing items away to "clean up"

D. Preserving information (notes/video) and minimizing unnecessary handling

48) Which report sentence is most objective?

A. "He was obviously guilty."

B. "She's always causing trouble."

C. "I observed the person walk past the point of sale holding unpaid merchandise."

D. "He did it on purpose because he's a criminal."

49) A visitor refuses a consent search. A professional response is to:

A. Force the search because it's private property

B. Detain them until they agree

C. Take their property as punishment

D. Follow procedure (for example, deny entry or ask them to leave)

50) A site policy requires a bag check for entry. If someone refuses, you

should generally:

A. Let them in anyway

B. Search their bag without consent

C. Threaten arrest for refusing the bag check

D. Deny entry and follow site procedure

51) Which is a strong de-escalation technique?

A. Matching the person's anger to dominate

B. Using a calm tone, listening, and giving simple choices

C. Making personal comments to "win"

D. Threatening force immediately

52) Which non-verbal behaviour is most helpful for reducing tension?

A. Pointing aggressively

B. Standing too close

C. Keeping hands visible and maintaining a safe distance

D. Blocking the person's path to prevent leaving

53) Which radio message is best?

A. "Come here now!"

B. "It's crazy—hurry!"

C. "Control, this is Patrol 2 at the south entrance. Disturbance in progress. Request assistance."

D. "You won't believe what just happened..."

54) Which is the best example of proper medical incident documentation?

A. "He was faking it."

B. "She had a heart attack, I'm sure."

C. "Person complained of dizziness. 911 called at 10:12. EMS arrived at 10:20."

D. "He deserved it for not listening."

55) Safety Data Sheets (SDS) are used to:

A. Show safety information about hazardous products
B. List employees scheduled for shifts
C. Provide court dates for trials
D. Explain radio call signs

56) If bodily fluids (blood) are present, the safest approach is usually to:

A. Handle it without gloves to save time
B. Follow procedure, use appropriate protection, and avoid unnecessary contact
C. Ignore it because it's not your job
D. Collect samples for evidence

57) Which action is most clearly unprofessional and risky?

A. Writing a factual report after an incident
B. Calling for backup early
C. Directing people calmly during an evacuation
D. Posting incident details and names on social media

58) The Court of Appeal for Ontario primarily:

A. Handles routine building alarms
B. Conducts first aid training
C. Issues security licences
D. Reviews decisions from lower courts when appealed

59) Which example is most likely a civil matter?

A. A person sues a business after slipping and being injured
B. An assault in a parking lot
C. Theft from a store
D. Mischief (property damage)

60) When you feel unsure on scenario questions, the best general test strategy is to choose the answer that:

A. Prioritizes safety, follows procedure, uses least force, and calls for help when needed

B. Sounds toughest and most aggressive

C. Avoids reporting to reduce paperwork

D. Focuses on punishment to “send a message”

17

Answer Key

Practice Exam #1 Answers

1. D — A security guard's core role is to deter, observe, report, and assist.
2. C — Professionalism is staying calm and following site procedure.
3. A — Accepting a gift to ignore a rule is a classic conflict of interest.
4. B — PSISA emphasizes licensing, professional conduct, and the Code of Conduct.
5. C — A guard's authority is mainly from citizen authority + property owner's rules.
6. D — A suspected weapon is a high-risk situation; call police immediately.
7. C — Citizen's arrest is limited and must meet legal conditions.
8. B — Suspicion alone (no reliable facts/observation) is not a safe legal basis to arrest.
9. C — Reasonable force is the least force necessary and appropriate to the situation.
10. C — Force becomes excessive when it continues after the threat is controlled.
11. A — Good assessment considers threat, environment, and available backup.
12. B — Consent searches require voluntary agreement.

13. C — If a person refuses a required entry condition, deny entry and follow procedure.
14. C — Detention means the person is not free to leave.
15. D — Don't touch suspicious packages; create distance and follow procedure.
16. B — Treat alarms seriously and support evacuation per the emergency plan.
17. C — Stay calm, gather details if possible, then notify per procedure.
18. A — Lockdowns are used when staying secured inside is safer than evacuating.
19. B — Call 911 (or direct someone to) and follow emergency procedure.
20. B — Duty to act = take reasonable steps, call help, follow procedure.
21. A — Good Samaritan principles support helping in good faith within your abilities.
22. C — Objective documentation states symptoms/actions and times, not diagnoses/opinions.
23. B — WHMIS is about communicating hazardous product information in workplaces.
24. C — Create distance, report, and follow procedure; don't handle unknown chemicals.
25. B — Slips/trips/falls are common real-world hazards for guards.
26. B — Strong reporting is factual: what/where/when/who notified/actions taken.
27. B — Calm, clear, respectful instructions are most effective and professional.
28. C — Crowding/pointing aggressively can escalate conflict quickly.
29. D — Radio messages should be brief, clear, professional, and accurate.
30. C — Professional language is neutral and direct without insults or threats.
31. B — Early intervention during tension is easier and safer than waiting for crisis.
32. C — Calm tone, listening, and simple choices are core de-escalation tools.

33. B — Cultural awareness = fair rules + respectful communication, no bias/assumptions.
34. B — Suspected weapon = create distance and call police immediately.
35. B — Reports matter because they create a record others may rely on later.
36. A — A DAR summarizes routine shift activities and notable events.
37. B — Legal-quality reports include timeline, location, observations, actions taken.
38. C — "Observed shouting/profanity" is observable behaviour (objective).
39. A — The 5 Ws ensure completeness: who/what/when/where/why.
40. C — Guessing and assumptions are a common (and damaging) report error.
41. C — Use notes/systems; state only what you can support (don't guess).
42. C — Criminal law involves offences against society prosecuted by the Crown.
43. B — Civil law typically involves disputes and compensation between parties.
44. A — Courts decide guilt/innocence and legal outcomes.
45. B — Police investigate crimes and enforce criminal law.
46. D — Corrections manages custody/sentences and supervision programs.
47. C — Security supports justice via prevention, observation, reporting, and escalation.
48. B — Reports contain sensitive info; share only with authorized people.
49. B — If it resolves peacefully, document and notify as required by procedure.
50. B — Start with calm verbal direction and space, not force.
51. C — Acknowledging emotion and inviting calm discussion is de-escalation language.
52. B — You can request ID, but if refused you follow site procedure (no forcing).
53. B — Mitigate (if safe/allowed) and report the hazard promptly.
54. B — Smoke + alarm = treat as real; trigger response and call for help.
55. B — Best practice is facts, actions, times, and outcomes—no opinions.
56. C — Best radio: identifies caller, location, situation, and request clearly.

57. A — Distance, boundaries, and early backup reduce risk and escalation.
58. C — A lawsuit for injury is typically civil law.
59. B — Follow access rules or ask a supervisor; don't do favours.
60. **C** — Best emergency approach: safety first, call help early, follow procedure, document.

Practice Exam #2 Answers

1. B — Core role is deterrence, observation, reporting, and assistance.
2. B — Safety + procedure + calm communication are the professional priorities.
3. C — PSISA emphasizes honesty, professionalism, and proper conduct.
4. C — Taking money to ignore rules is unethical and corrupt.
5. A — You generally must be properly licensed to work as a guard in Ontario.
6. A — Carry required ID/licence and present it when appropriate per policy/law.
7. D — Impersonating/appearing like police is prohibited and misleading.
8. A — Guard arrest power is generally limited like a citizen's arrest.
9. A — Section 494 is the key citizen's arrest section.
10. A — After arrest: call police promptly and follow procedure; don't "interrogate."
11. B — Reasonable force = least necessary and appropriate for the circumstances.
12. C — Proportionality = response matches the threat level.
13. B — Continuing force after control is achieved is excessive.
14. A — Continuum guides selecting the least-forceful effective option.
15. A — Assessment includes threat, environment, weapons risk, backup, etc.
16. C — Consent search requires voluntary agreement.
17. A — If refusal: explain policy and follow procedure (often deny entry).

18. B — Guards have limited seizure powers; follow policy and involve police when needed.
19. A — Don't touch; create distance, keep people away, follow procedure.
20. C — Stay calm, gather details if possible, then notify per procedure.
21. B — Support evacuation and follow the emergency plan; don't assume false.
22. C — Lockdown is for situations where staying secured inside is safer.
23. A — Call 911 (or direct someone to) and follow procedure first.
24. D — Bring/use AED promptly and follow prompts/training.
25. D — Duty of care: act reasonably to prevent harm and follow procedure.
26. C — WHMIS communicates hazards of workplace products via labels/SDS.
27. B — Report hazards promptly with facts and correct notifications.
28. C — Good prevention: safe footwear, alertness, avoid unnecessary risk.
29. A — Best radio includes who/where/what/what you need.
30. B — Neutral, clear, respectful direction is professional.
31. D — Acknowledges emotion + invites calm problem-solving.
32. D — Tension stage shows frustration, raised voice, refusal to cooperate.
33. C — Apply rules fairly; communicate respectfully without bias/assumptions.
34. A — Safety-first: distance, boundaries, early backup.
35. D — "Observed" behaviour is objective and report-appropriate.
36. D — 5 Ws = who/what/when/where/why.
37. D — Guessing motives/assumptions is a common error.
38. A — Legally sound reports are factual, clear, and time/location/action-based.
39. A — Criminal law covers offences against society prosecuted by the Crown.
40. B — Courts decide guilt/innocence (and legal outcomes).
41. D — Security supports justice through prevention, observation, reporting, escalation.
42. B — Reports contain sensitive info; share only with authorized people.
43. C — Without direct observation/evidence: gather facts, notify, police if

appropriate.

44. D — Follow procedure; keep distance; involve police if required for removal.
45. C — Most guard roles prioritize safety, warning others, and calling police early.
46. B — Early backup + distance reduces risk and escalation.
47. D — Preserve notes/video; minimize handling; follow procedure.
48. C — Objective: observable actions (past point of sale with unpaid items).
49. D — If consent refused: follow procedure (deny entry/ask to leave).
50. D — Required condition refused: deny entry and follow procedure.
51. B — Calm tone, listening, and simple choices are key de-escalation skills.
52. C — Visible hands + safe distance signals non-threat and reduces tension.
53. C — Best: clear ID, location, situation, and request.
54. C — Objective symptoms/actions/times; no diagnosis or judgment.
55. A — SDS provide safety/handling info for hazardous products.
56. B — Follow procedure; use PPE; avoid unnecessary contact with bodily fluids.
57. D — Posting names/details online breaches professionalism/confidenti ality.
58. D — Court of Appeal reviews lower-court decisions on appeal.
59. A — Injury lawsuit is typically civil law.
60. **A** — Best strategy: safety, procedure, least force, call help early, document.

VIII

QUICK REVIEW & EXAM DAY

18

Quick-Study Cheat Sheets

This chapter is designed for fast review. Use these cheat sheets the week of your exam, or anytime you want a quick refresher before a shift. They are not meant to replace a complete study—to help you remember the most testable points.

Powers of Arrest Summary

Big idea: Security guards do **not** have police powers. Most arrest authority comes from **citizens' arrest** rules and must be used carefully.

You MAY consider an arrest when:

- You **directly observe** a criminal offence being committed (or the legal conditions for a citizen's arrest are clearly met)
- There is a **clear safety reason** or an immediate need to act
- You can do it **safely**, and **backup** is available when needed
- You plan to **contact the police immediately** and follow the site procedure

You should NOT arrest when:

- You have only **suspicion** (no clear facts)

- The person only broke a **site rule** (not a criminal offence)
- The risk is high (weapons suspected, large group, unsafe environment)
- You are acting out of **anger**, embarrassment, or "punishment."
- You cannot explain your grounds clearly and calmly

After an arrest (high-level):

- Call the police **as soon as possible**
- Use only **reasonable force** if required for safety
- Keep the situation controlled and professional
- Document a clear **timeline** and actions taken

Use of Force Dos and Don'ts

Big idea: Force must be **reasonable**, **proportional**, and used only when necessary. Stop when the threat stops.

DO

- Use presence and communication first when possible
- Keep a safe distance and maintain an exit route
- Call for backup early if the risk is increasing
- Use the **least force necessary** for the shortest time necessary
- Stop using force once the person is controlled or danger is over
- Document what happened clearly and factually

DON'T

- Use force to punish or "teach a lesson."
- Escalate because someone is rude or insulting
- Continue force after control is achieved
- Take unnecessary risks (especially if weapons are suspected)
- Use threats, insults, or aggressive body language

- Guess or exaggerate in your report

Exam reminder: If an answer sounds angry, punitive, or ego-driven, it's almost always wrong.

Trespass Rules

Big idea: Private property owners can set access rules. Security helps enforce those rules fairly and safely.

Key points:

- Sites can set **entry conditions** (sign-in rules, restricted areas, bag checks, etc.).
- If someone refuses a condition of entry, the usual response is: **deny entry**
- If someone is told to leave and refuses, it may become a **trespass issue**
- Removing someone physically is risky—often the safest option is to create space and **call the police**, depending on the procedure

What to do in a typical trespass situation:

1. Stay calm and professional
2. Give a clear direction: "You must leave the property."
3. Explain consequences: "If you refuse, police may be called."
4. Keep a distance and call for backup if needed
5. Document what was said and done, including times

What not to do:

- Argue or escalate
- Make threats you can't legally carry out
- Use force unless lawful, necessary, and safe

Report Writing Checklist

Use this checklist to make your reports strong, clear, and exam-ready.

Before you write:

- Review your notes and confirm key times
- Organize events in order (timeline)
- **Include the "5 Ws":**
- **Who:** involved persons, witnesses, responders notified
- **What:** what happened (facts), what you observed directly
- **When:** date and times (key events, police/EMS arrival)
- **Where:** exact location (building/area/room)
- **Why:** why you took actions (based on safety and procedure)

Write like this:

- Use facts and observations ("I observed...")
- Use simple, clear sentences
- Keep tone professional and neutral
- Record actions taken and outcomes

Avoid this:

- Opinions ("He was guilty")
- Diagnoses ("heart attack") unless confirmed
- Guessing, exaggerating, or using emotional language
- Slang, insults, or jokes

Final check before submitting:

- Would someone understand what happened without asking you questions?

- Is the timeline clear?
- Did you record what you did and who you notified?

19

Exam Day Preparation

Exam day feels stressful for many people. The most effective way to reduce stress is to prepare your plan in advance. This chapter covers what to bring, how to manage your time, common traps, and what typically happens after you pass.

What to Bring

Bring what you need so you are not distracted or delayed.

Bring these basics:

- Government-issued photo ID (the same type required by your test provider)
- Your exam booking confirmation or registration details (paper or digital)
- A simple watch (optional, if allowed)
- Any approved items listed by the testing provider (follow their rules)

Also recommended:

- Water (if permitted)
- A light snack for after the exam

- A jacket or sweater (test rooms can be cold)

Do not bring (or do not use):

- Notes, textbooks, or study sheets
- Unauthorized electronic devices
- Anything the exam provider says is not allowed

If you are unsure, check the exam provider's instructions before you go.

Time Management Tips

Most people lose marks not because they don't know the content, but because they rush, panic, or overthink.

Use this simple method:

1. **First pass:** Answer the easy questions quickly.
2. **Skip and mark:** If you're unsure, choose "skip," mark it, and move on.
3. **Second pass:** Return to the harder questions with more time.
4. **Final check:** Review skipped questions and confirm you answered everything.

Other useful tips:

- Read the question first, then look at the answers.
- Watch for words like **"best," "first," "most appropriate," "must,"** and **"should."**
- Avoid spending too long on one question early in the exam.

Common Exam Traps

Many exam questions are designed to test judgment. They often include answer choices that sound confident but are unsafe or unlawful.

Common traps include:

- **The "tough guy" answer:** aggressive, threatening, punishment-focused
- **The "shortcut" answer:** skipping procedure, skipping reporting, ignoring policy
- **The "assumption" answer:** guessing facts not given in the question
- **The "police power" trap:** acting like you can search, detain, or arrest freely
- **The "too much force" option:** using physical control when communication would work
- **The "vague" option:** unclear actions like "handle it" without steps

A strong exam answer usually includes one or more of these ideas:

- Safety first
- Call for help early when needed
- Follow the procedure and post orders
- Use the least force necessary
- Write accurate notes and reports

What Happens After You Pass

Passing the exam is an important step, but it is not the final step. After you pass, you typically still need to complete the licensing process before you can legally work as a security guard.

What usually happens next:

- You apply for your Ontario security guard licence through the proper provincial process
- You submit the required documentation and fees
- You wait for your licence to be issued/approved
- Once licensed, you can work as a security guard (and must follow PSISA standards)

Keep copies of your training and exam records. Also, remember that rules and processes can change over time, so always follow the current Ontario requirements.

Final Exam-Day Tip

If you get stuck on a scenario question, choose the answer that is:

- **Safe**
- **Legal**
- **Professional**
- **Procedure-based**
- **Uses the least force necessary**

This approach will guide you to the best answer in most exam situations.

IX

APPENDICES

These appendices are designed to help you review quickly, prepare your paperwork, and find official Ontario information when you need it.

20

Appendix A: Frequently Asked Questions

1) Is this book enough to get licensed?

No. This is a study guide to help you prepare. Ontario licensing also requires training, testing, and an application process.

2) Where do I book the Ontario security guard test?

Ontario uses an official testing site (Serco/DriveTest system). It explains booking, locations, online vs in-person options, and what you need to book.

3) How long is the test and what format is it?

The official booking site states the test is **90 minutes** and **multiple-choice**.

4) What is a Training Completion Number (TCN)?

Your TCN is your ID number connected to training/testing and is used for licensing purposes.

5) How much does the test cost?

The booking site lists **$35.00 + HST** (total shown as **$39.55**) and notes fees can change. This is current as of December 2025.

6) Can I cancel or reschedule my test?

The official booking site states appointments are final and test fees are not refundable; it also links to their cancellation policy.

7) What documents do I need to apply for the licence?

The Ontario application package (individual) lists common requirements such as: a **CRJMC** from a police service (issued within the last **6 months**), **two pieces of government ID** (with specific purposes), a **passport-quality photo**, and payment (method depends on how you apply).

8) Where do I apply for the licence?

Ontario provides an online Licensing Portal (and also mail-in options exist in the application package).

9) What laws matter most for the exam?

Expect many questions tied to PSISA expectations, Code of Conduct, arrest authority (Criminal Code), trespass authority in Ontario, use-of-force reasonableness, emergency response, and report writing. PSISA and the Code of Conduct are official Ontario sources.

Made in the USA
Monee, IL
04 November 2026

67385536R10095